7-24-21

Junior High School Library
Bremen, Indiana

Nappanee, IN 46550

582
Gui

Title 2

66-94

A TREE IS BORN

BY
J. M. GUILCHER
AND
R. H. NOAILLES

Sterling Nature Series

STERLING PUBLISHING CO., INC.
New York

STERLING NATURE SERIES

A TREE IS BORN

A FRUIT IS BORN

A BIRD IS BORN

A BUTTERFLY IS BORN

A BEE IS BORN

AN ANT IS BORN

1965 Printing

Revised Edition, 1964

Published in the United States of America
by Sterling Publishing Co., Inc.
419 Fourth Avenue, New York 16, N. Y.

Manufactured in the United States of America

CONTENTS

Introduction	9
The Horse Chestnut Tree	13
The Oak Tree	45
The Walnut Tree	61
The Pine Tree	77

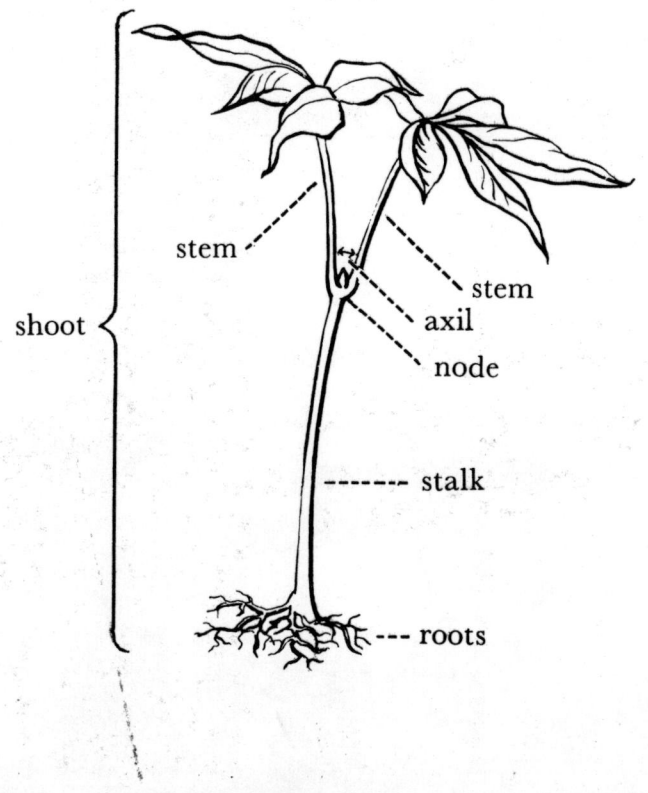

With the approach of winter all living things are filled with a strange feeling of anxiety. In late autumn the animals feel the coming of cold and hunger. Each faces the threat in its own way: by migration—traveling to warmer lands; by hibernation—sleeping throughout the winter in a protected nook; or by resistance—fighting for survival.

The swallow flies off to the south. The lizard buries itself deep under the pebbles. The dormouse nibbles its last nuts before going to sleep for long months in its grass-lined nest.

Plants can neither migrate nor struggle to stay alive. They have only one choice—to suffer and to endure if possible. The poppy dies, its seeds scattered on the ground. The daisy keeps only a fringe of leaves at ground level which the first slight snowfall will cover. The lily, primrose and iris leave no trace at all above ground; they withdraw into tuber or underground stalks.

Trees are more robust. Only their leaves are weak. Those of the pine tree are tough and hard, covered with a thick skin. Those of the horse chestnut and the oak are soft and delicate. If the leaves were to stay on the tree, frost would destroy them and open up wounds through which germs would penetrate deep into the tree's body. But the leaves fall with the first frosts and the point where each broke off is covered by a weatherproof scar tissue. Now the tree is ready to face the winter.

Its life slows down daily. Its roots no longer draw water from the ground. Sap no longer rises rapidly through its trunk. Breathing becomes slower. In November, the oak still has a few wisps of dry, brown and shriveled leaves. The horse chestnut is simply a huge plucked carcass. They both seem to be dead.

But they are only asleep. Deep in their thousands of buds the leaves and flowers of approaching spring are already forming. Acorns and nuts that have fallen in the autumn from the oak and horse chestnut lie dormant on the ground. In each a tiny plant is waiting, well protected by the seed coat. Winter storms may sweep up dead leaves, twist branches, dash boughs against each other, but everything is in place for the awakening of spring.

From February on, life is at work. Seeds buried in the ground begin to grow; the hazel blossom blows with the wind. With warmer days, each week has its surprises. In March there are the first birds in the valleys, the pussy willows, the flowers in the orchards. And the horse chestnut buds swell, soon to burst open. In April the whole forest springs to life. The sap rises, buds burst, branches are covered with new leaves, all fresh, tiny and crinkly. Everywhere insects are born or awaken, eager to live, anxious to lay their eggs. The birds build their nests and call their companions. It is mating time again. The wind sways the oak tree's catkins; the pine tree releases its sulphur-colored pollen; the bee brings to the horse chestnut pistils the living dust that will fertilize them. In the leaf mold below the tree, the seeds have shaken off their drowsiness. The horse chestnut and the acorn split their tarnished skins. Thousands of plants take root, thousands of slender stalks reach for the light. Life takes over once again.

After the great upsurge of spring, growth gradually slows down. In summer, the branches disappear beneath thicker foliage. Flowers fade; one by one the withered petals fall into the grass. Fruits swell slowly. Soon the new shoots will stop growing.

The fine days go on—seemingly without end—as a scaly bud takes shape at each leaf axil, the point between the leaf stem and the stalk from which it springs. The newborn oaks are still attached to the acorns that feed them, and yet a bud is already sprouting from the top of its stalk. The days grow shorter as autumn approaches. The dusty leaves are gnawed by insects. Here and there the foliage shows a yellowish tinge. In a few more weeks the first dead leaves and the first chestnuts will fall together. Summer is over. Flights of migratory birds fly high across the sky. The life of the tree is going to be interrupted by winter once more.

The Horse Chestnut

In winter the horse chestnut looks dead.

In spring its buds burst open from the pressure of sap.

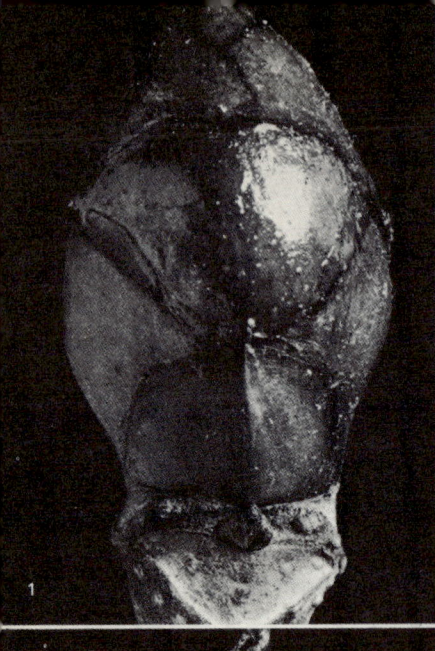

1. OUTSIDE VIEW OF A BUD IN WINTER
2. SECTION OF A LEAF BUD

(magnified 3 times)

Illus. 1. Here is the terminal bud that grows on the end of a stalk. Its hard scales overlap like shingles on a roof. They are coated with a sticky substance which gives them a shiny look.

All horse chestnut buds have the same appearance, but their contents are not all the same. Some will produce a stem with leaves, others a stem bearing flowers.

Illus. 2. This bud contains the outline of a stem. Its first leaves are so small, so folded, so wrapped in a cottony fuzz that they cannot be seen clearly.

The stiff brown scales are folded over soft, pale green, interwoven scales. This scaly envelope protects the delicate tissues of the young shoots—the new stems with their leaves or flowers—from dampness and cold.

The next 8 photographs show the growth of a leaf shoot.

Leaf buds contain the outline of

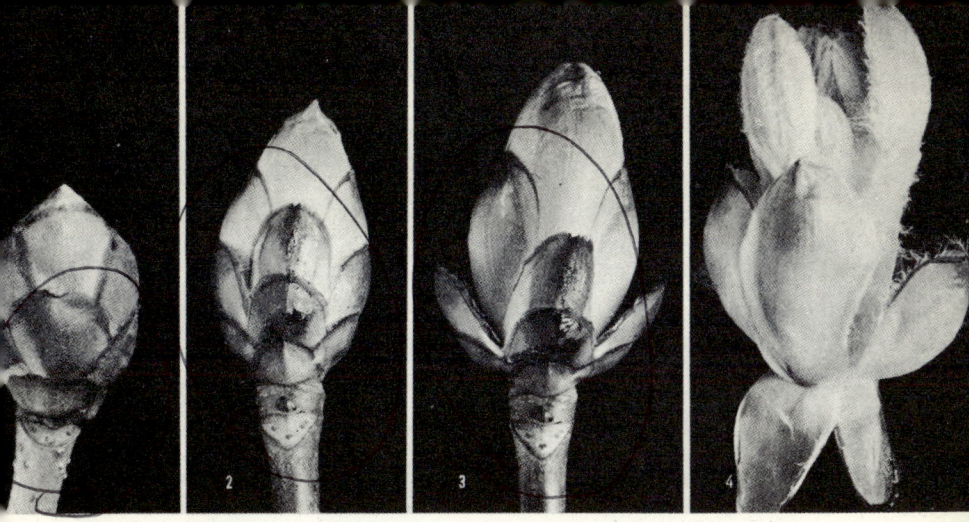

1 to 7. OPENING OF A LEAF BUD IN SPRING
DEVELOPMENT OF THE LEAF SHOOT

Illus. 1. Toward the end of March the bud swells. Fed by the flow of sap the tiny stem, hidden behind the scales, has already grown bigger.

Illus. 2. The hard scales loosen their grip. The inside scales, still soft, grow longer, together with the stem which is still invisible.

Illus. 3. The hard scales fold back toward the stem. The soft scales have reached their maximum size. They will open when their time comes.

Illus. 4. The young leaves appear at last above the coverings of the bud. They are still very small and covered with fuzzy hairs. They do not yet look like fully grown leaves.

a leaf stem. Their scales open . . .

17

Illus. 5. Stem and leaves grow bigger. A branch, delicate-looking yet hardy, seems to burst from the scales of the bud, growing longer and fuller each day.

The leaflets of each leaf are still stuck together.

Illus. 6. The stem grows still longer. The leaves unfold their leaflets. The tip of the shoot goes on producing new tissues. Tiny young leaves appear. They all seem to be attached at the same place, but in a few days the growth of the stem will space them out, two by two, with each pair at a different level.

The scales of the bud (at the bottom of the picture) begin to wither. They will soon drop off.

the tiny stem begins to grow; the

leaves expand and spread their leaflets.

Every branch has a leafy shoot

LEAF SHOOTS IN SUMMER

Each fully grown shoot reaches a different height.

Illus. 7. This shoot is long, and has several levels of widely spaced leaves.

Illus. 8. This one is short and bears three pairs of leaves quite near each other. The place where the bud first formed the shoot is clearly seen below the lowest pair of leaves. The bud scales have fallen off, leaving narrow scars on the stalk. Together these scars form a ring. There is a similar ring toward the bottom of the picture. This is where the terminal bud was the year before. The space between the two rings represents last year's shoot. The number of these "year rings" tells us the age of a branch. The young shoots of this year's growth already bear winter buds.

at the end, which lengthens it.

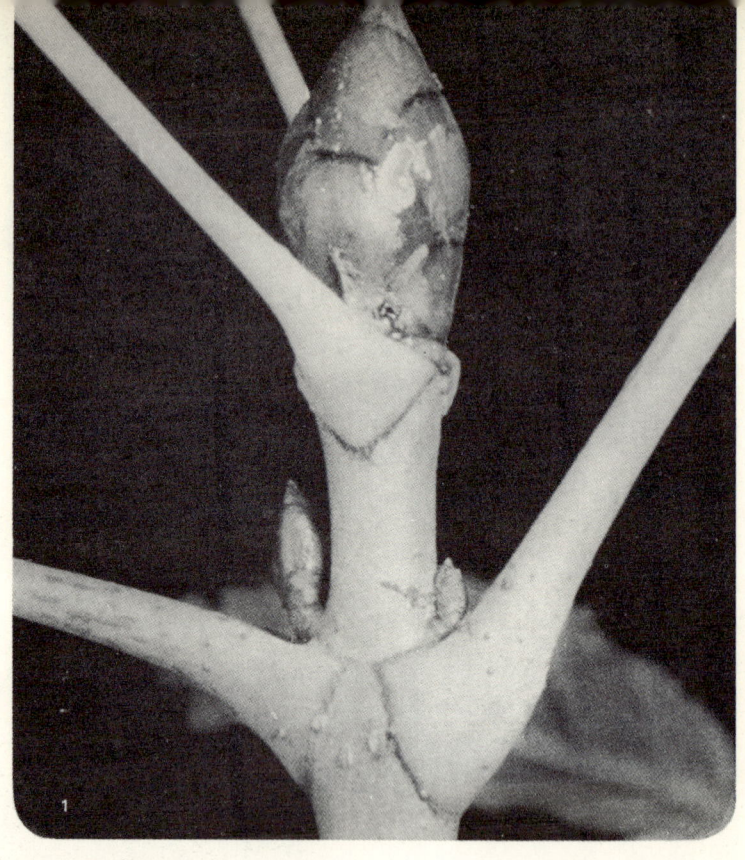

Illus. 1. Here is the tip of the shoot shown on page 21. Leaf stems, not side-growing (lateral) branches, are growing out from the stalk. When its growth is complete, the young shoot has new buds that can face the coming winter. The very big bud at the top is the terminal bud, and the smaller ones at each leaf axil are the lateral buds. Next spring the terminal bud will lengthen the branch, and some lateral buds will extend it outward. (Not all of the lateral buds develop. Some remain undeveloped for years.)

The shoot produces new buds which will

1. TIP OF A LEAFY SHOOT IN SUMMER
2 and 3. LEAVES FALL IN AUTUMN

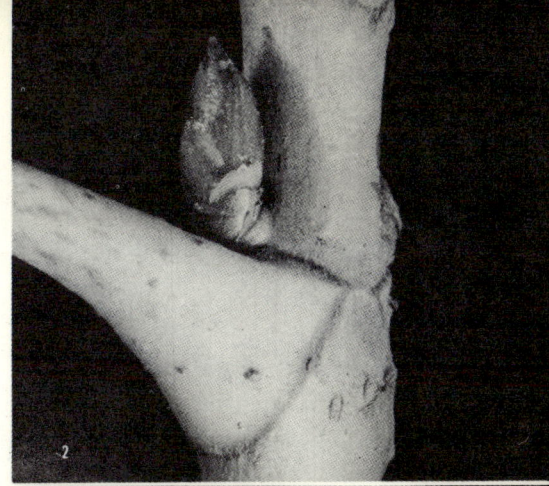

When autumn begins, the leaves turn yellow, dry up and fall.

Illus. 2. Here is the base of a leaf stem and the bud formed at its axil. A cork-like partition has already formed at the point where the leaf stem joins the main stalk. When the leaf is completely dry, the first puff of wind will carry it away.

Illus. 3. The leaf falls and reveals the corky scar. In the scar and in the fallen leaf stem we can see the ends of the channels through which the sap has flowed during the spring and summer. Leaf scars, bud scales and the stalk covering all give continuous protection to the new shoot. Dampness and frost cannot get at it.

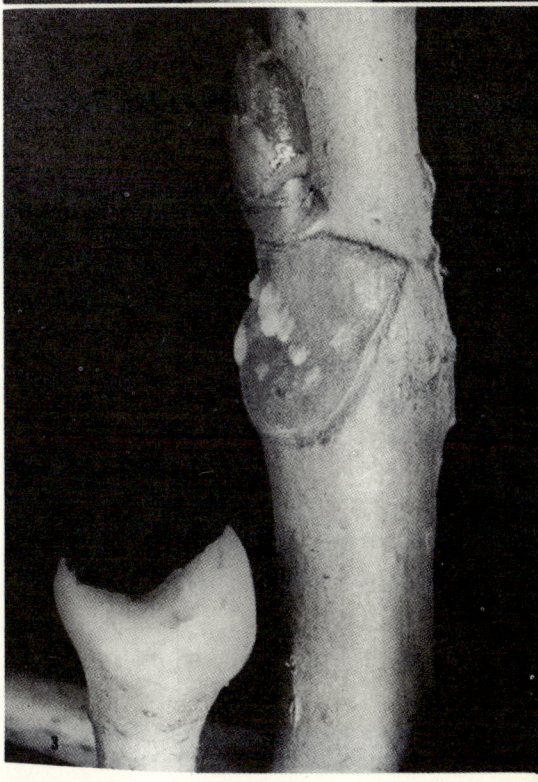

remain on the stalk after the leaves fall.

23

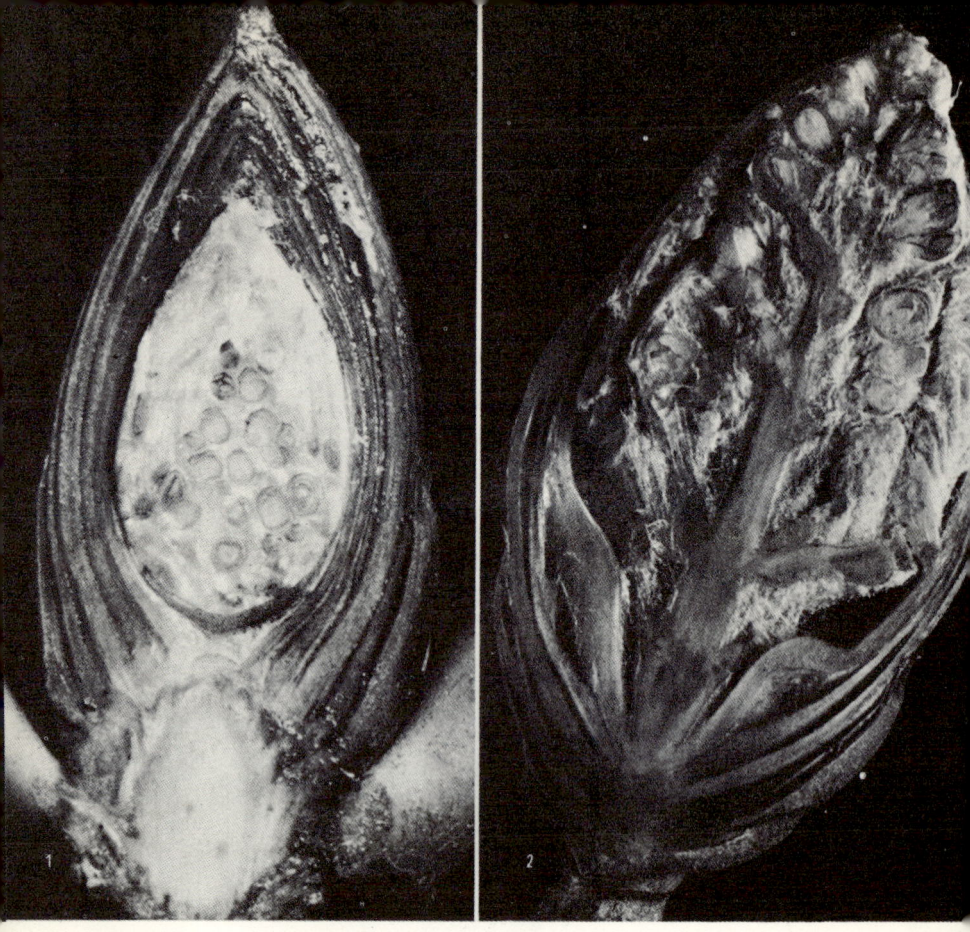

(magnified 5 times)
1. SECTION OF A FLOWER BUD IN AUTUMN
2. SECTION OF A FLOWER BUD IN SPRING

From autumn on we can see the immature flower buds in a cutaway section of the bud (Illus. 1). But it is only at the end of winter that the future shoot will take on something like its mature form (Illus. 2). We can now

The "flower" buds release

3. THE OPENING OF FLOWER BUDS

recognize the stem and the flowers in its upper part. Everything grows bigger. The inner scales get larger, and so does the cluster which the scales still hide. In a few days the bud opens (Illus. 3).

a tiny, compact cluster.

1 and 2. DEVELOPMENT OF FLOWERING SHOOTS

From each bud there grows a rather short stem with some leaves and a tiny cluster of flower buds. In a few weeks this reaches its full size. The stem of the cluster grows longer; the buds, at first crowded together, spread out so their individual stems grow longer. The flowers open. They are usually white, speckled with red and yellow. Certain species of horse chestnut have red flowers. Now the plundering insects come. They plunge into the corollas (the petal formation) to suck nectar, and in going from flower to flower they carry pollen from one to the other.

The cluster stretches out, rising above the

leaves, and opens into white or red corollas.

At first glance all the flowers in a cluster seem alike, with their waving corollas and their curved stamens. Actually there are two kinds. Most flowers have only stamens, as in Illus. 2.

Many flowers have only stamens.

1. HORSE CHESTNUT IN FLOWER (opposite page)
2. CLUSTER OF MALE FLOWERS
3. SECTION OF A BISEXUAL FLOWER

(magnified 1½ times)

These are male flowers. Others are bisexual (Illus. 3), with a pistil which ripens early, and stamens which develop a little later. These flowers are female first and male afterward. A curved "style," ending in a slender stigma, arises from the ovary.

Others have a pistil and stamens.

1. AFTER POLLINATION, THE BLOSSOMS WITHER AND FADE
2 to 5. THE FERTILIZED PISTIL CHANGING INTO FRUIT

Illus. 1. Here the flowers have fallen, the corollas have faded. It looks as if a catastrophe has struck the withered cluster.

Illus. 2. Petals and

The flowers fade. Here and there a fertilized

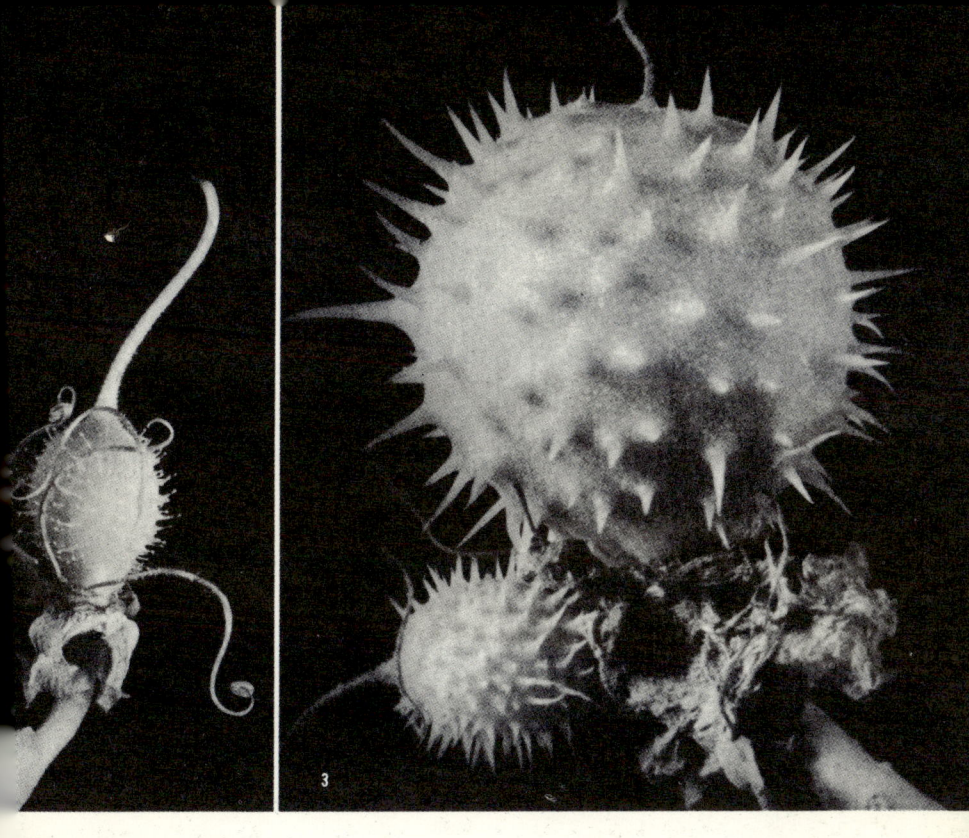

3

stamens have dried up. Only the pistil remains. The ovary has soft, fleshy prickles. It has grown bigger. (Compare it with Illus. 3 on page 29.)

Illus. 3. Some weeks later the ovary turns into this large round fruit, bristling with stout prickles. We can still recognize the remains of the withered corolla at its base and the remains of the shriveled style on top.

pistil remains and changes into a fruit.

In October the ripe fruit falls to the ground,

Illus. 4. Six ripe fruits, six prickly cases, are all that remain of the cluster of beautiful flowers. First, cracks appear in their surface; then the cases open, fall and release their seeds. A bud has grown at each leaf axil. When the whole cluster has fallen from the stalk and when the leaves have also fallen, the tip of the branch will appear as shown in the inset. The following spring each of these two terminal buds will produce a new shoot, either leaf-bearing or flower-bearing, and the branches will develop in a forked formation.

Illus. 5. A case has just dropped to the ground and opened into three segments. The seeds have shiny, veined skin.

where it bursts open to release its seeds.

1. A HORSE CHESTNUT SEED
2. A SECTION OF THE SEED
3. THE EMBRYO PLANTLET IN DETAIL

Illus. 1. Each chestnut is a huge seed, covered by a brown, weatherproof skin. The light patch on the surface is a scar, showing where the seed was originally attached to the fruit. The seed germ looks white within the skin.

Illus. 2. Like all seeds, the horse chestnut contains a plant in the embryonic or undeveloped stage. The white, floury mass, filling almost the whole seed, will become the first two leaves—called the cotyledons. They are so misshapen by the reserves of food packed within their tissues now that they do not look much like leaves. The pointed part of the embryo, separated from the cotyledons by an infold of skin, will become the root of the embryo.

Illus. 3. The axis of the embryo is made up of the radicle and plumule with rather a vague region between. The two cotyledon leaves extend from the sides of this axis. Everything together makes up the embryo. At the tip of the plumule are tiny, undeveloped foliage leaves that look like a small feather. That is why the part is called a plumule (meaning, like a plume). The embryonic little plant will be nourished by the food reserves stored in the cotyledons.

Each seed contains the beginnings of a whole

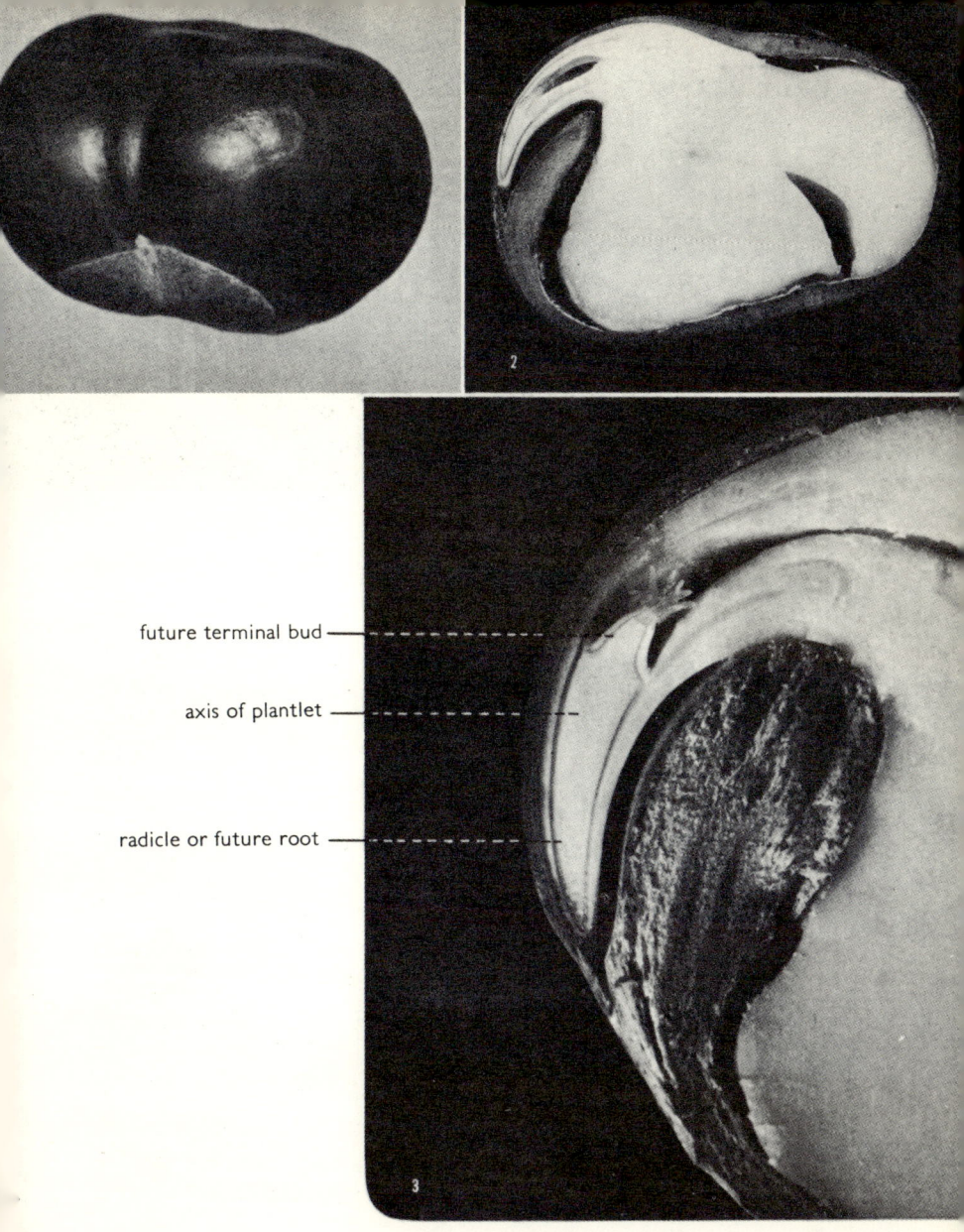

future terminal bud
axis of plantlet
radicle or future root

(magnified 5½ times)

plant supplied with a mass of food reserves.

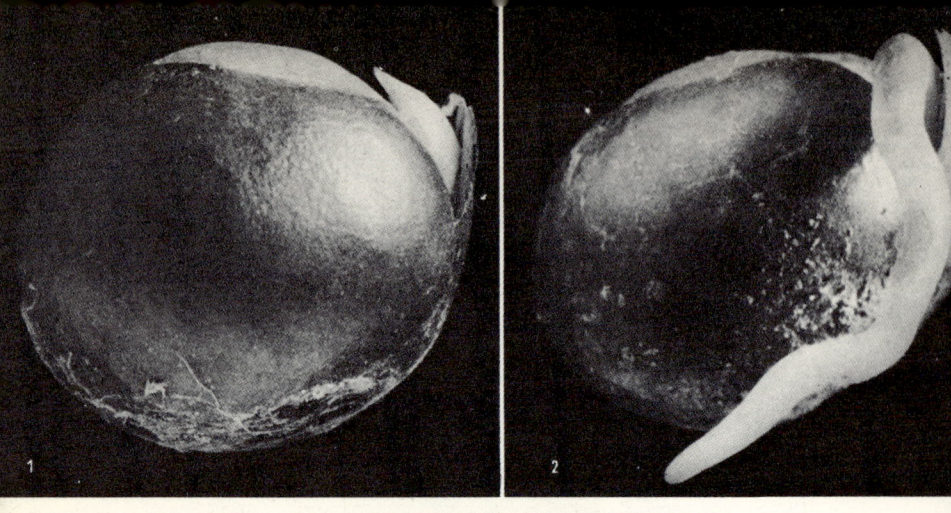

1 to 10. GERMINATION AND DEVELOPMENT OF THE EMBRYO

The seed spends the winter with the tempo of its life slowed down—it is asleep. It sprouts or germinates in spring when the ground it lies on is aerated, damp, and warm enough. Photographs 1 to 5 show seeds and plantlets that have been taken from the soil. The later illustrations show specimens that have taken root.

Illus. 1. The seed absorbs water from the earth; it swells. The seed coat, dull and shriveled after its winter in the soil, now is stretched by the pressure within. The embryo begins to grow. The skin breaks at a weak spot, and the radicle presses outward.

Illus. 2. The young root grows, fed by reserves in the seed. Avoiding the light and attracted by the soil, it stretches downward and penetrates into the earth.

Winter over, the horse chestnut seed germinates.

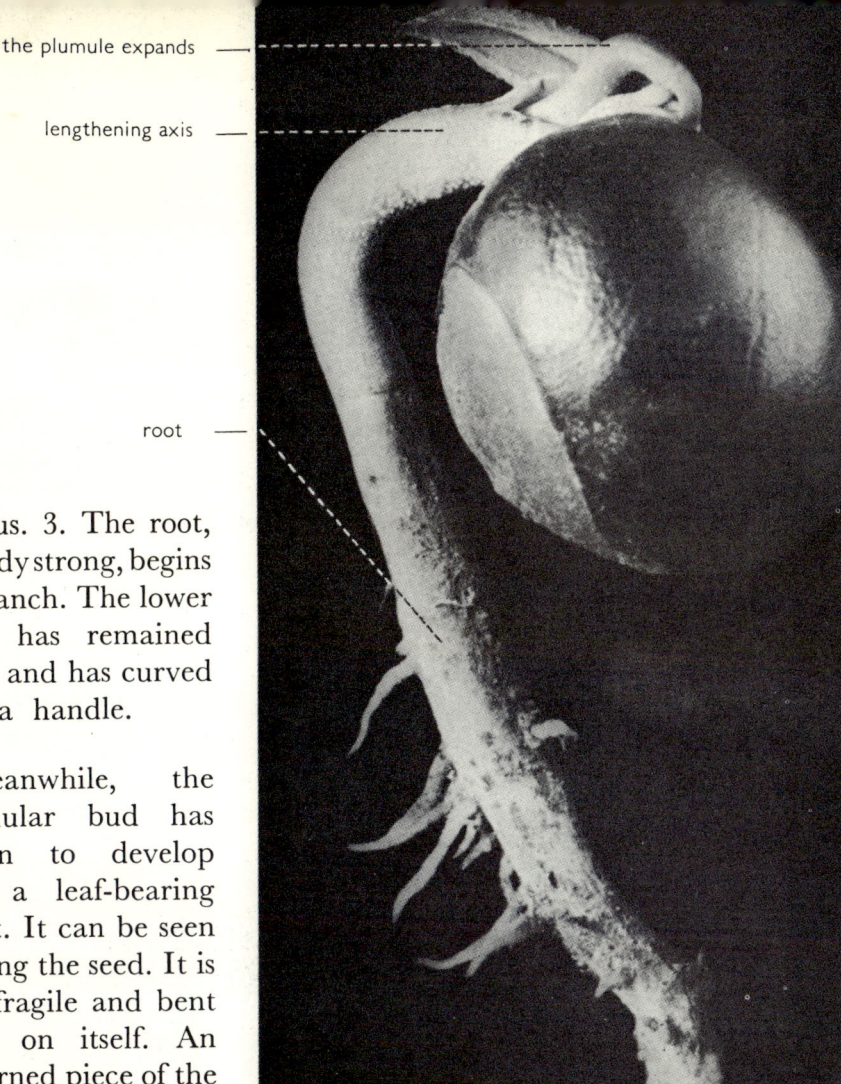

the plumule expands

lengthening axis

root

Illus. 3. The root, already strong, begins to branch. The lower stem has remained short and has curved like a handle.

Meanwhile, the plumular bud has begun to develop into a leaf-bearing shoot. It can be seen leaving the seed. It is still fragile and bent back on itself. An upturned piece of the broken seed coat is in back.

The plantlet sinks its root into the ground.

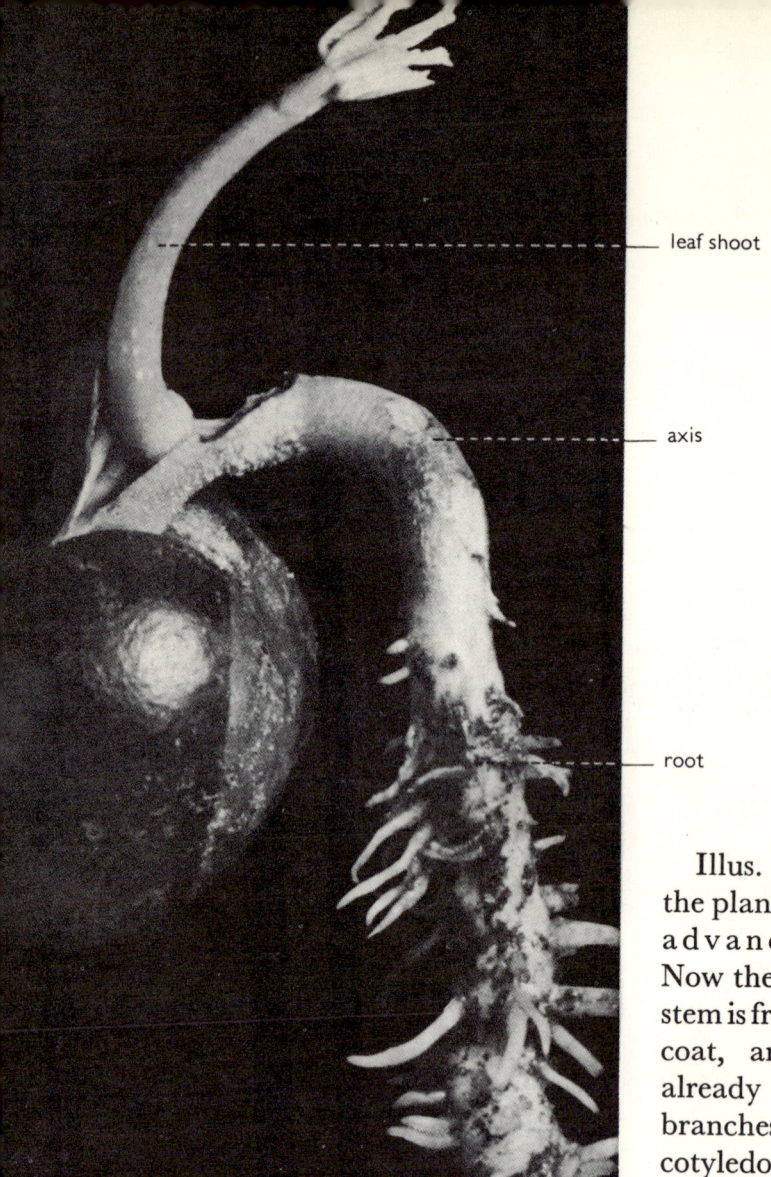

Illus. 4. Here is the plantlet at a more advanced stage. Now the leaf-bearing stem is free of the seed coat, and the root already has many branches. So only the cotyledons remain enclosed in the seed.

The root lengthens and branches.

the shoot

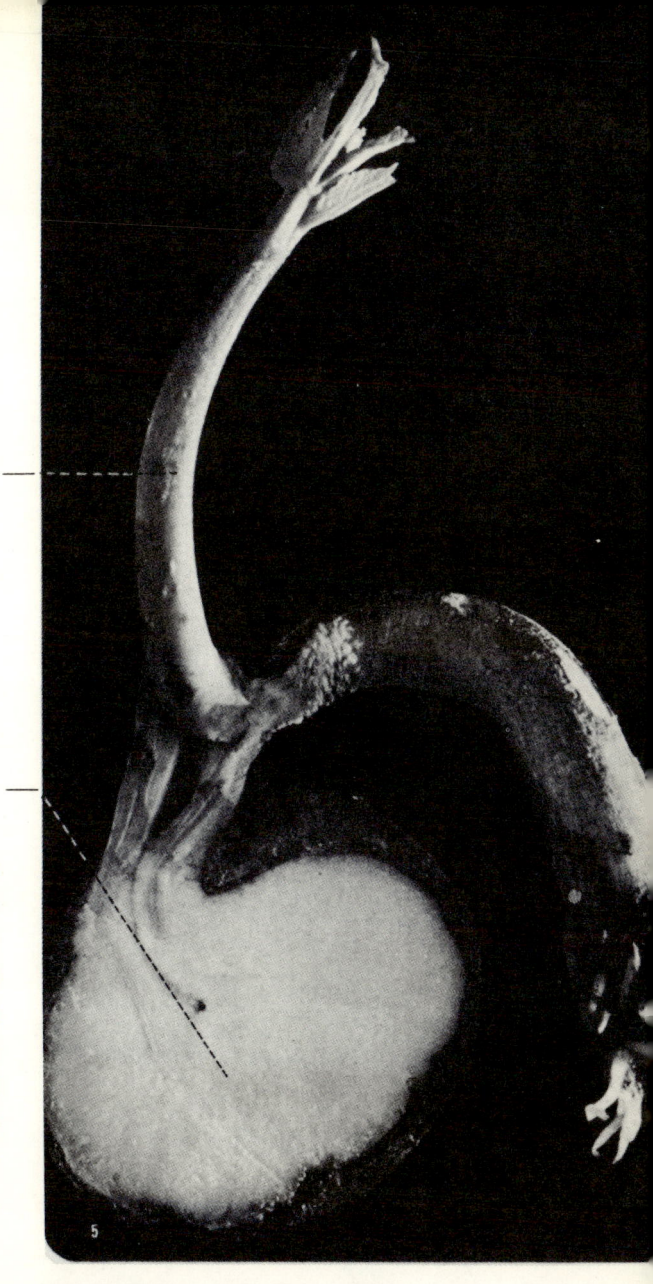

cross section of the cotyledons

Illus. 5. This picture shows in cross section the cotyledons, still stuffed with food reserves although they have, up till now, provided all the food needed for the growing plantlet.

The leaf-bearing stem frees itself from the seed.

Illus. 6, 7 and 8. The stem straightens and grows longer. At its top end, two leaves grow and spread their leaflets. These leaves are in every detail like the leaves of the full grown tree.

With the small root pushing down into the earth and the shoot stretching up toward the light, the tiny horse chestnut tree grows taller. By the end of the first year the shoot may be two or three feet high. Although it is still connected to the cotyledons in the half-buried seed, it is now able to nourish itself.

Straight and slender, it soon

spreads its first two leaves.

9. A HORSE CHESTNUT SEEDLING BY THE AUTUMN OF THE FIRST YEAR
10. ITS TERMINAL BUD
11. THE SHOOT IN THE SECOND YEAR

Illus. 9 and 10. Toward the end of summer the tiny horse chestnut tree stops growing. A winter bud, wrapped in hard scales, forms at the tip of its stem, between the two shoots.

Illus. 11. The following spring this bud produces a new shoot which lengthens that of the previous year. It bears leaves at many levels. A bud will form at each leaf axil, another at the tip of the branch.

From year to year, from terminal bud to terminal bud, the young tree will become taller and taller. At the same time, by the development of lateral buds, it will throw out branches. Only after about twenty-five years will it become fully mature and flower in its turn.

A winter bud forms between the shoots.

When spring comes it will make the stalk grow.

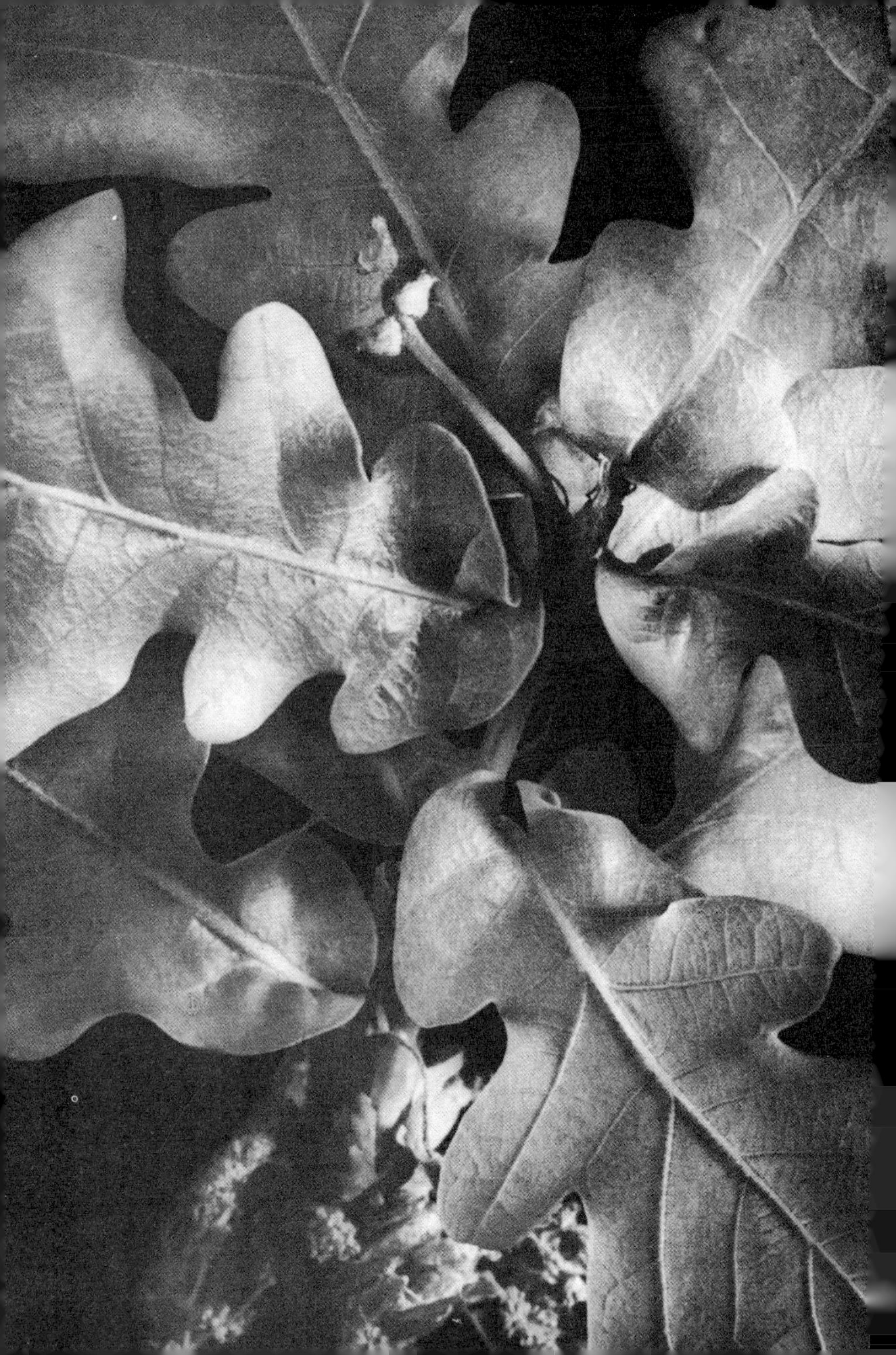

THE OAK TREE

1. AN OAK BRANCH IN SUMMER
2. A BUD READY TO OPEN

The oak tree is one of the biggest and loveliest of our trees. Look at the oak in the forest with its straight trunk and lofty branches. Observe the solitary oak with its dense foliage rounded like a dome. Its lobed leaves have a characteristic oak shape. In autumn they turn yellow, dry up and die. Sometimes the dry brown leaves remain attached to the branch for most of the winter.

The buds, with their short wide scales arranged in five rows, are also characteristic.

The following photographs show two successive stages in the opening of the buds in spring.

All alike in appearance,

(magnified 10 times)

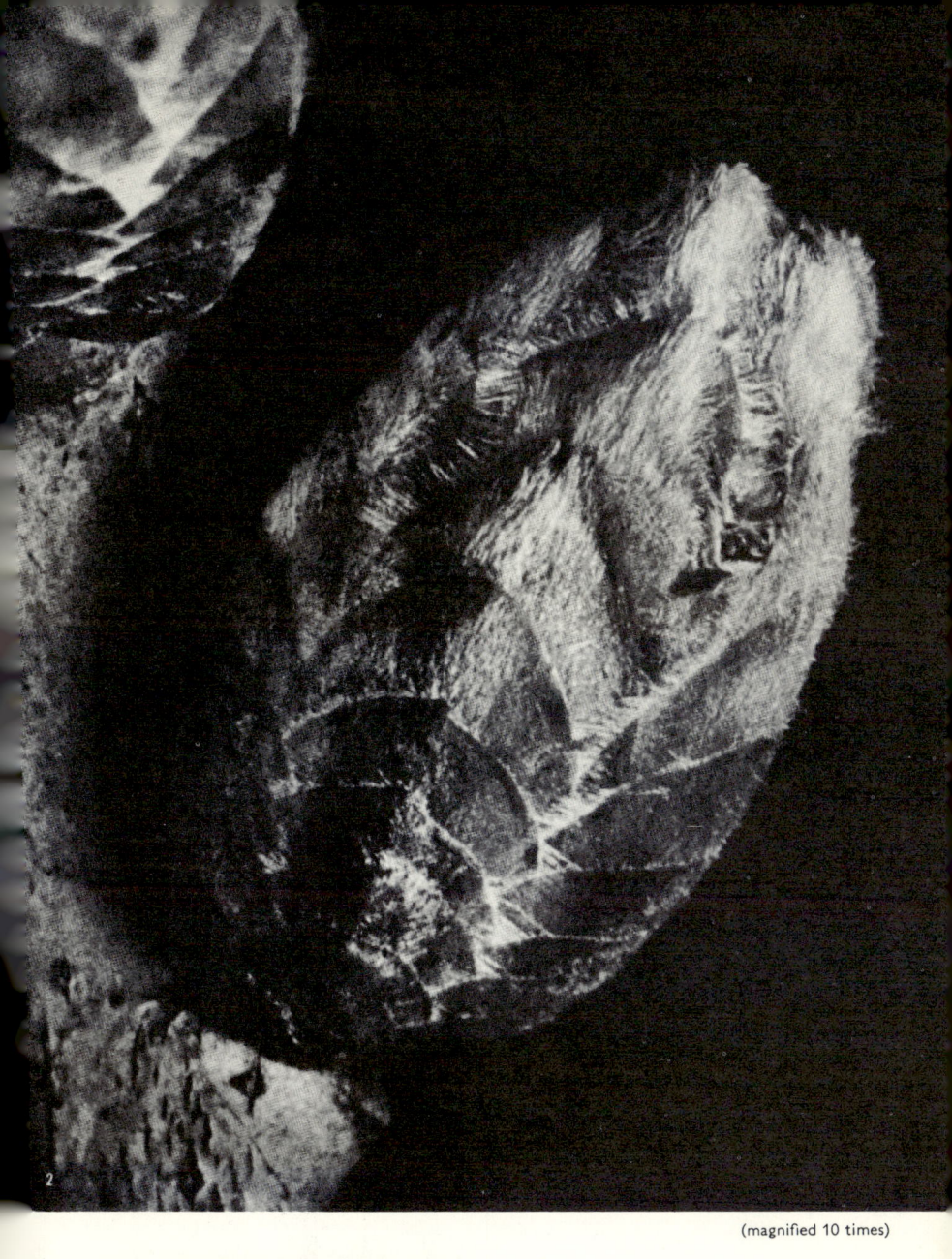

some buds of the oak tree . . .

. . . produce leaf and flower shoots;

DEVELOPMENT OF
NEW SHOOTS

The lower buds have now produced only catkins — slender, hanging shoots with flowers arranged in circles. These catkin flowers are male. From the upper bud is growing a leafy shoot with flowers. At its base hang male catkins, while above can be seen a little cluster of female flowers.

others produce only male flower catkins.

49

1. MALE FLOWER CATKINS

The flowers of the oak tree do not look like flowers at all; often they are not even noticed. They are small with no corolla.

Male and female flowers are separated and form quite distinct blossoms.

The male blossoms form in long, hanging catkins (Illus. 1). Each flower has five to ten stamens and some very narrow striped sepals. The female flowers (Illus. 3) are grouped in clusters of four or five. Their

The flowers, lacking corollas, are almost

2. MALE FLOWERS
3. FEMALE FLOWERS

structure is hard to make out. The rounded ovary is hidden by a whorl of many tiny scales. It supports a short, thick style with a flat, three-lobed stigma at its top.

These flowers are not attractive, have no scent or nectar, and are not visited by insects. It is the wind which carries the plentiful, light pollen from the male flowers over to the female flowers.

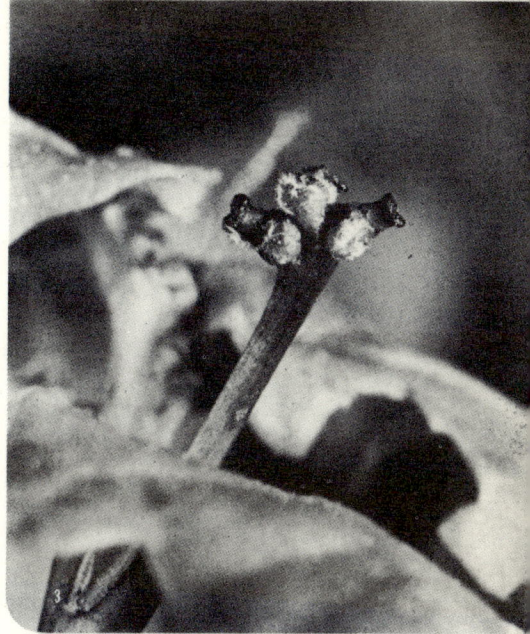

(magnified 6 times)

reduced to their reproductive organs.

1 to 4. THE FEMALE FLOWER PRODUCES A FRUIT

During the spring after fertilization, the pistils of the female flower are fertilized and develop into a dry fruit, the acorn. The ovary originally contained many ovules, but only one remains, so that the ripe fruit encloses only one seed.

Illus. 1. Here two very young acorns are attached to their common stem. (Do not mistake them for the winter bud at the top of the branch.) Their styles and stigmas have withered and only dry stubs remain. The ovary begins to swell. It is still wrapped in the cup which grows with it. The scales of the cup fit tightly over each other.

Illus. 2. The cup grows more slowly than the acorn, whose upper part sticks out more and more.

Illus. 3. Only the base of the acorn is now set in its cup. The cup has become woody and hard; the edge of the scales is no longer well defined.

Illus. 4. The ripe acorn is shaped somewhat like a melon. The parallel circles on its surface show the different levels that the rim of the cup reached. The base of the acorn detaches itself from its cup and now a knock or a puff of wind will be enough to separate them completely.

The growth of thousands of these fruits uses up the reserves of the tree. That is why an oak tree does not have acorns every year. "Acorn years" occur every two or three years, with years of little or no fruit-bearing between them.

The female flowers, each set in a

scaly cup, gradually become . . .

. . . acorns. In autumn the ripe acorn detaches

itself from the cup and falls to the ground.

1. A RIPE ACORN
2. AN ACORN WITH THE FRUIT WALL REMOVED TO SHOW THE SEED

The acorn is a dry, thin-skinned fruit, containing only one large seed. The fruit does not open: the seed remains enclosed until it germinates. Its only inner covering is a thin membranous skin (Illus. 2) which could not protect it.

This skin surrounds an embryo whose two cotyledons

The seed enclosed in the acorn contains

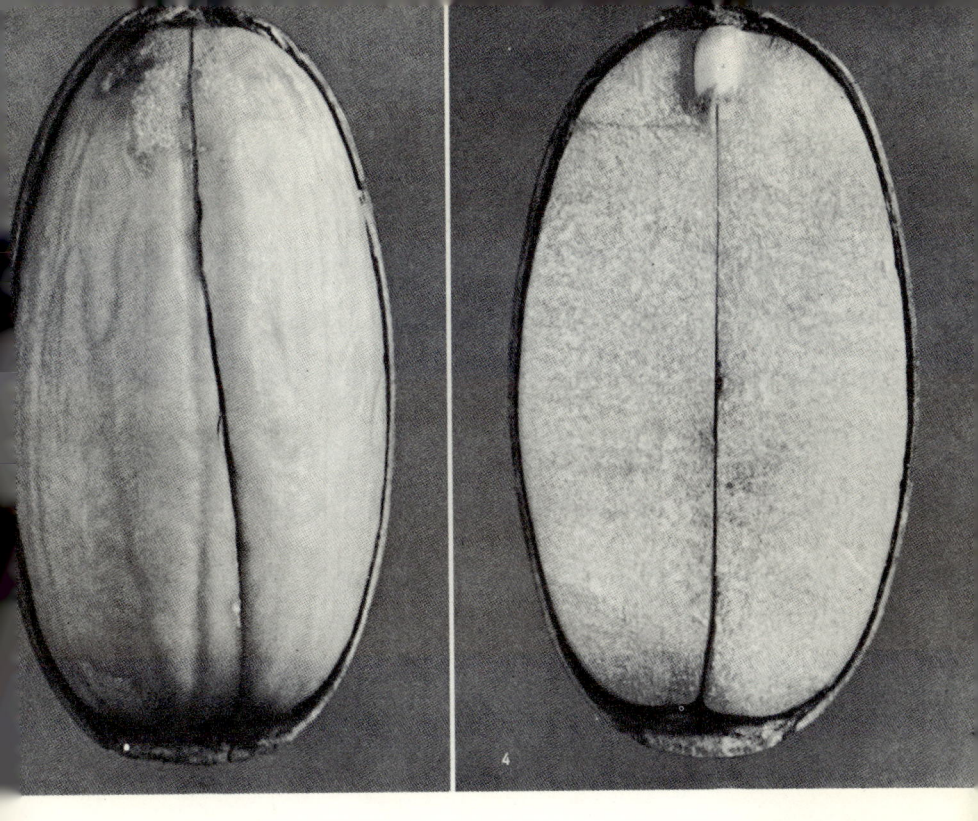

3. THE SEED WITH ITS COVERING REMOVED
4. SECTION OF THE SEED CUT TO SHOW ITS TWO MASSIVE COTYLEDONS AND THE AXIS OF THE EMBRYO

—the two first leaves—are swollen and deformed by food reserves like those of the horse chestnut. At first glance, they alone can be seen (Illus. 3). To reveal the other parts of the embryo, the seed must be split vertically (Illus. 4). Then the organs—radicle, axial region and terminal bud—can be seen but they are still difficult to identify.

an embryo rich in food reserves.

1. GERMINATION OF ACORNS IN SPRING
2 to 4. STAGES IN GERMINATION

Acorns fall to the ground in autumn and germinate the following spring. (Some begin to germinate as soon as they fall, but their growth soon stops, and is not resumed until the warm days come again.)

Generally, the oak's germination is similar to that of the horse chestnut:

The seed swells, bursting the skin of the fruit; the radicle begins to sprout (Illus. 2). It grows longer and buries itself in the ground. It has already become a very long root by the time a leaf shoot, the size of a tiny stump, finally emerges from the seed (Illus. 3 and 4). The acorn remains at the base of the new oak tree at least through the first year.

The acorns germinate. The plantlet frees itself from the seed. In a few more weeks

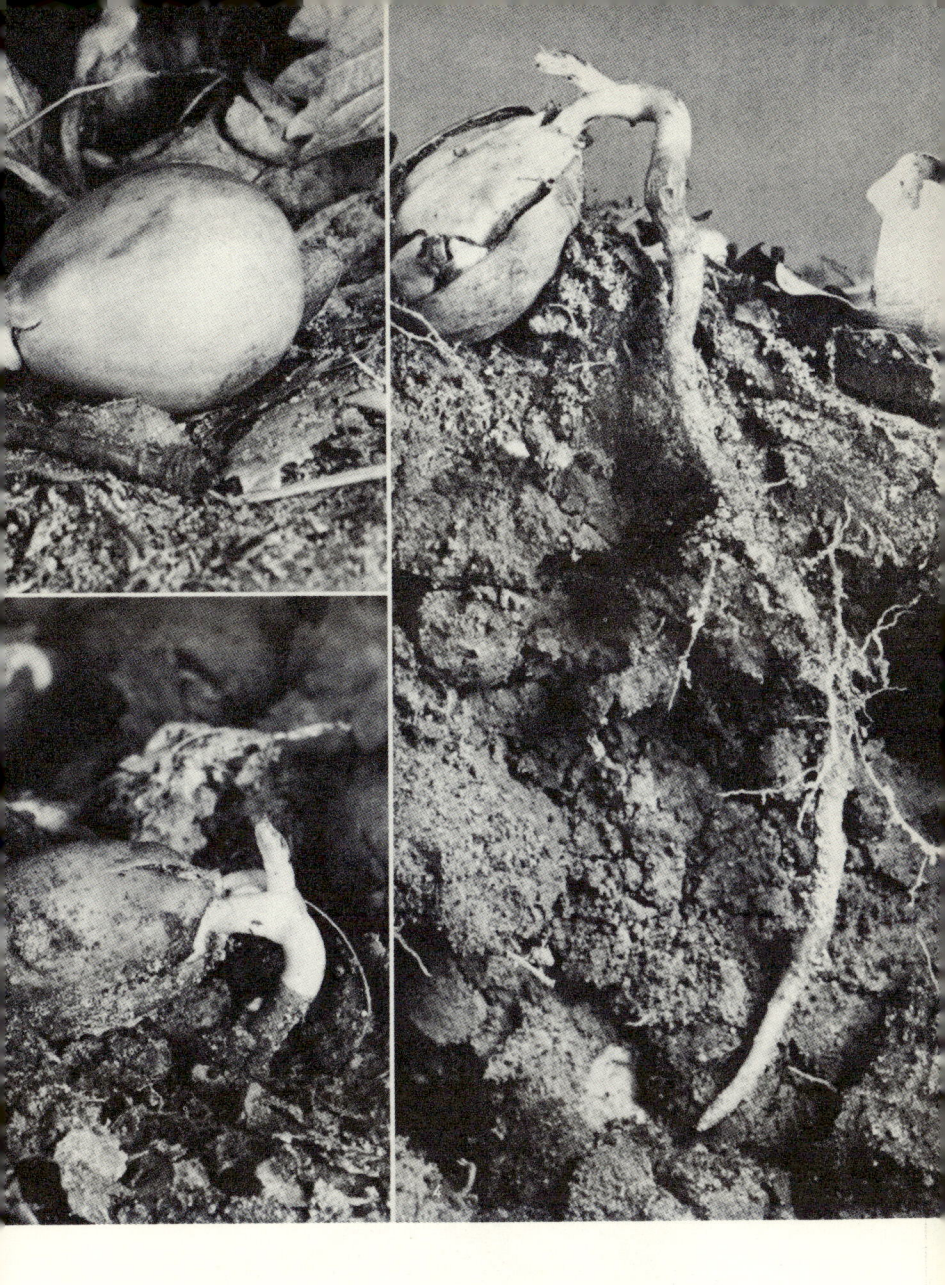

a tiny oak stretches its leaves to the light.

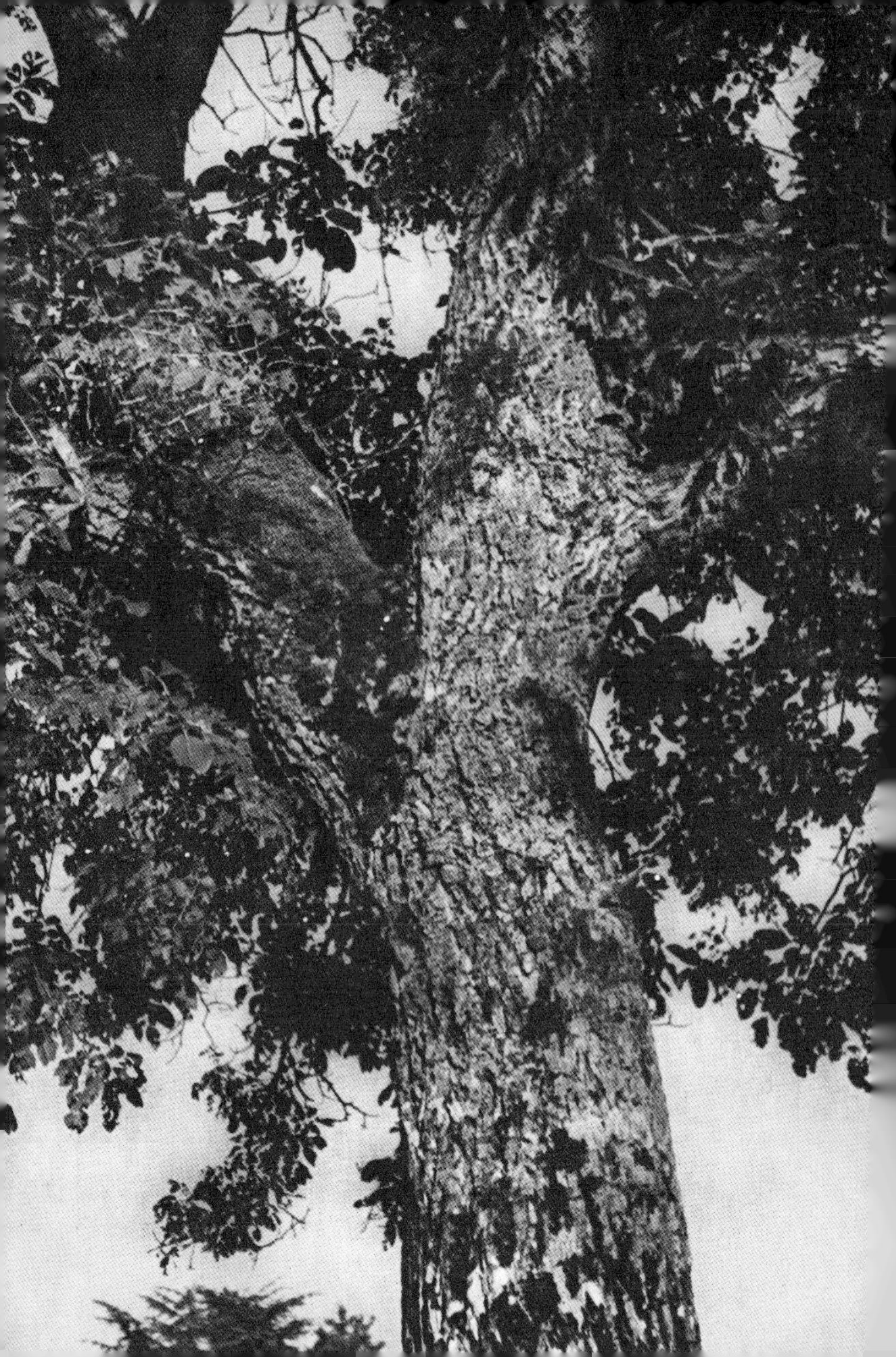

THE WALNUT TREE

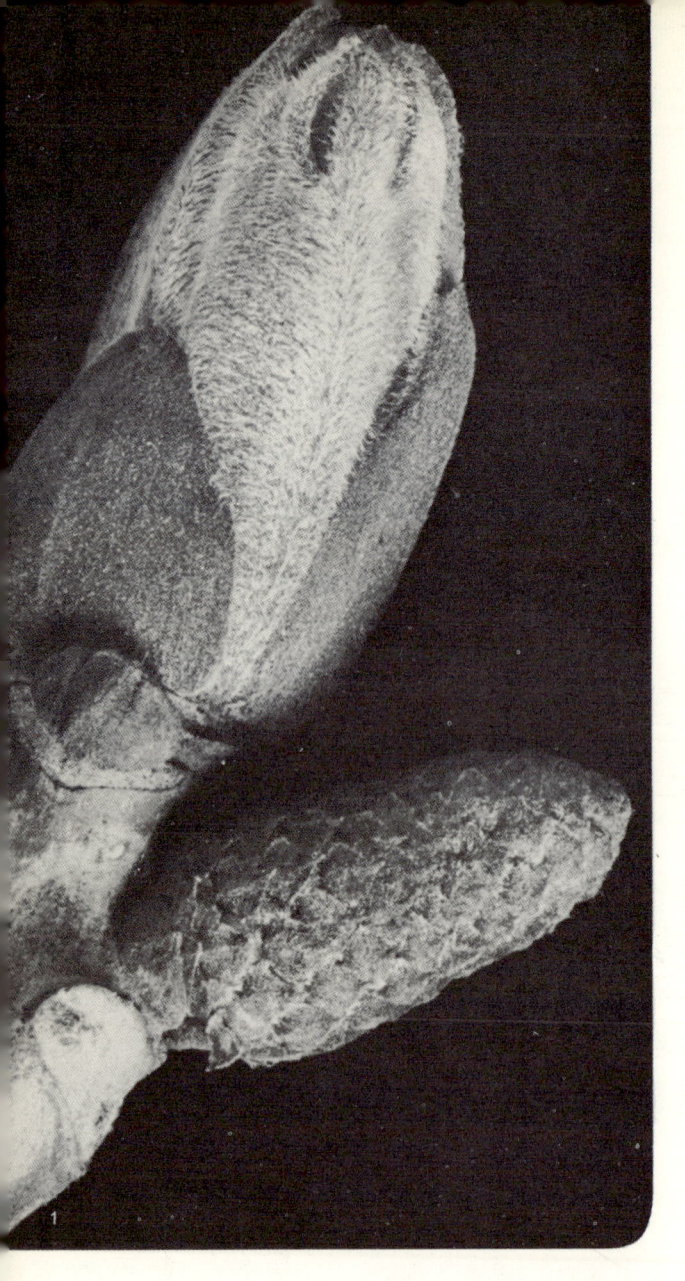

1. TWIG OF A WALNUT TREE IN EARLY SPRING
2. GROWTH OF THE YOUNG SHOOTS

Illus. 1. The buds of the walnut tree differ in content and appearance.

This terminal bud, for example, is enclosed in big furry scales; it will produce leafy shoots, and later, female catkins. The bud lower down on the branch has many small scales; buds of this type will produce only a catkin of male flowers.

The walnut tree has two kinds of buds.

Illus. 2. Compare the photograph on the right with the one above. The scale is the same in both pictures so we can measure the change that has taken place in a few days.

The terminal bud has opened. Its scales are at the base of the already long, leafy shoot. The axis of the catkin has grown longer and we can now see the flowers beginning.

Some form leafy shoots, others form catkins.

The leafy shoots bear female flowers.

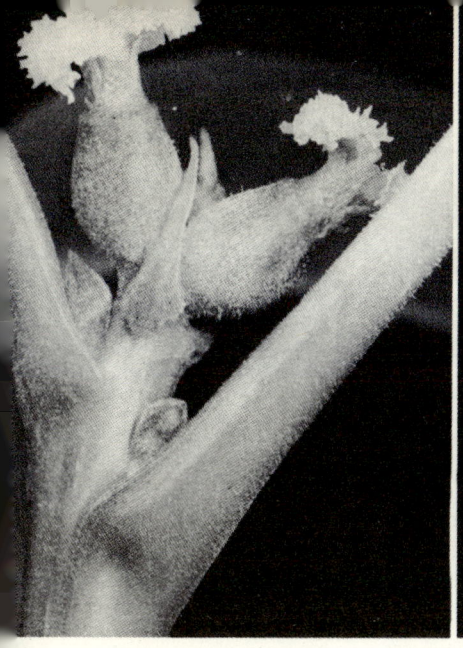

(magnified 3½ times)

1. BRANCH WITH LEAVES AND CATKINS
2. CLOSE-UP OF FEMALE FLOWERS
3. DETAIL OF A MALE CATKIN

Illus. 1. A few weeks later; the flowers and leaves have reached their full size. Female flowers—there are two in the upper left corner—appear on the leaf shoot. The catkins of male flowers hang down, attached to the branch that grew the year before.

Illus. 2. The flowers are very simple. The female flower has a large ovary which supports two stumpy styles, each with a thick stigma.

Illus. 3. Each scale of the catkin shelters a male flower that consists only of stamens. In the picture the unopened flowers are light in color; those that have burst open and lost their pollen are dark.

The catkins are composed of male flowers.

1 to 3. FORMATION OF THE FRUIT

The female flowers of the walnut tree, like those of the oak, are pollinated by the wind. The hairy surfaces of the stigmas catch the passing pollen grains. The fruit soon begins to form. The stigmas wither. The ovary grows bigger; it becomes a green walnut with a fleshy skin. In the meantime, new buds appear on the stalk. They are clearer on the following pages.

Pollinated by the wind, the female flower

becomes a plump fruit, a green walnut,

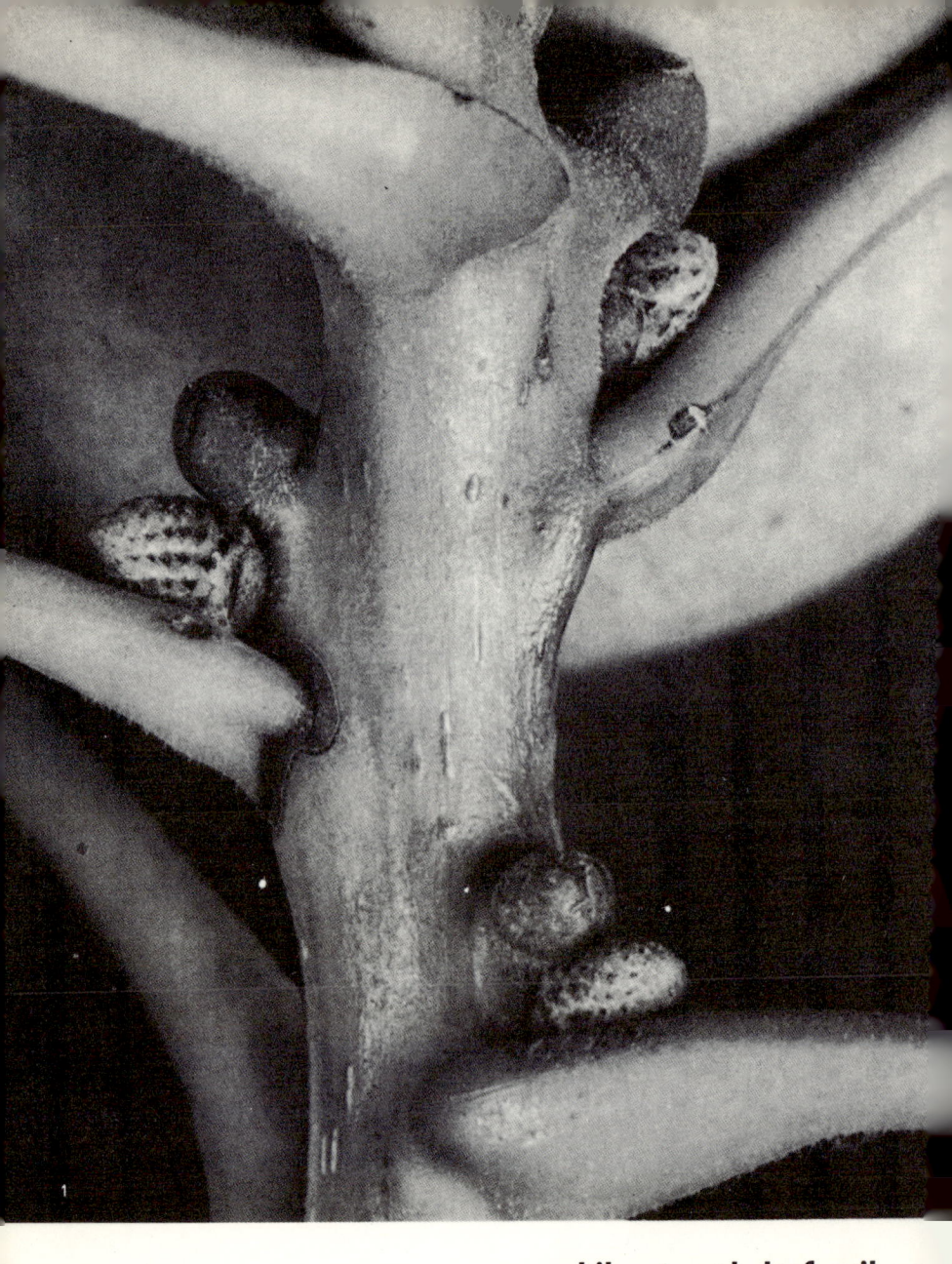

while at each leaf axil

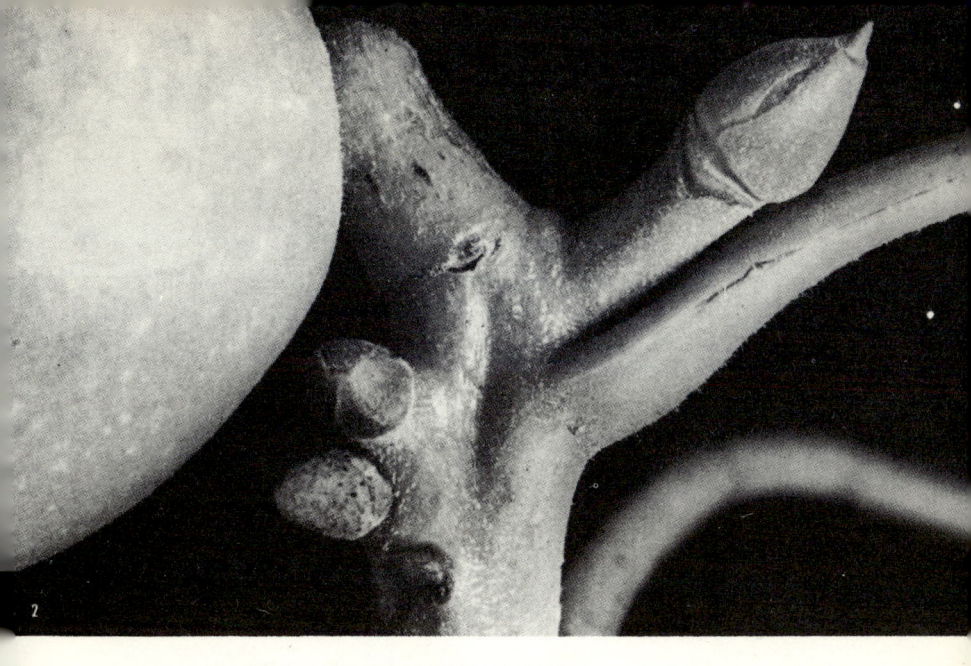

1 and 2. CLOSE-UP OF A NEW SHOOT IN SUMMER

Illus. 1. Here is the upper part of the stalk. Above and in the background is the green walnut.

Leaf stems are springing out from the stalk. There are two buds at the axil of each of them—a dark bud with large scales, which will produce a leaf shoot bearing female flowers, and a bud with many tiny scales which will become a catkin of male flowers.

Illus. 2. This picture, taken from a different angle, shows the relationship of a walnut to the terminal bud. The leaf bud, growing out sideways, was once a lateral bud, but is now assuming the function of the terminal bud which was suppressed by flowering.

two new buds are formed.

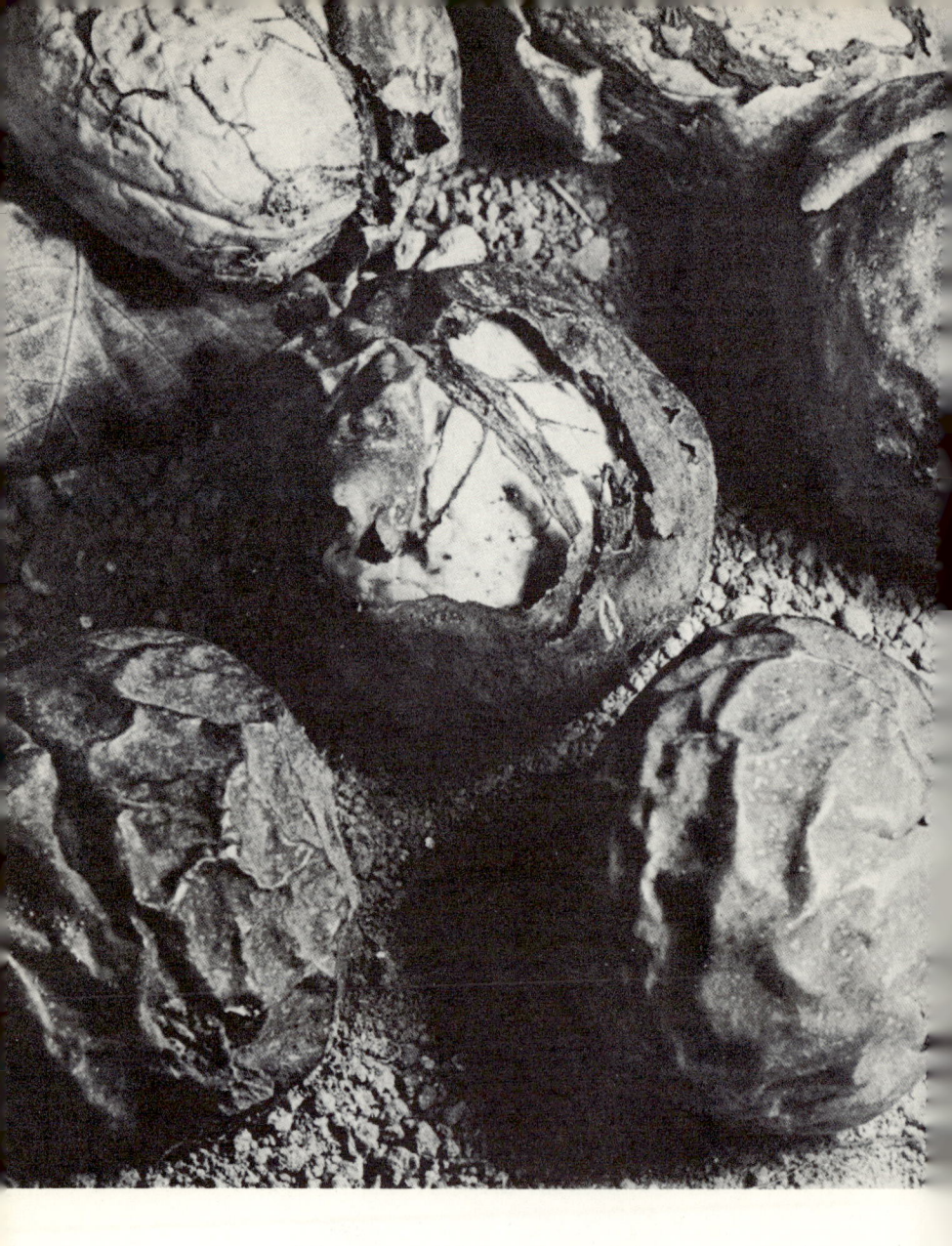

The green skin of the fruit rots away and

a fruit stone appears: the dry walnut.

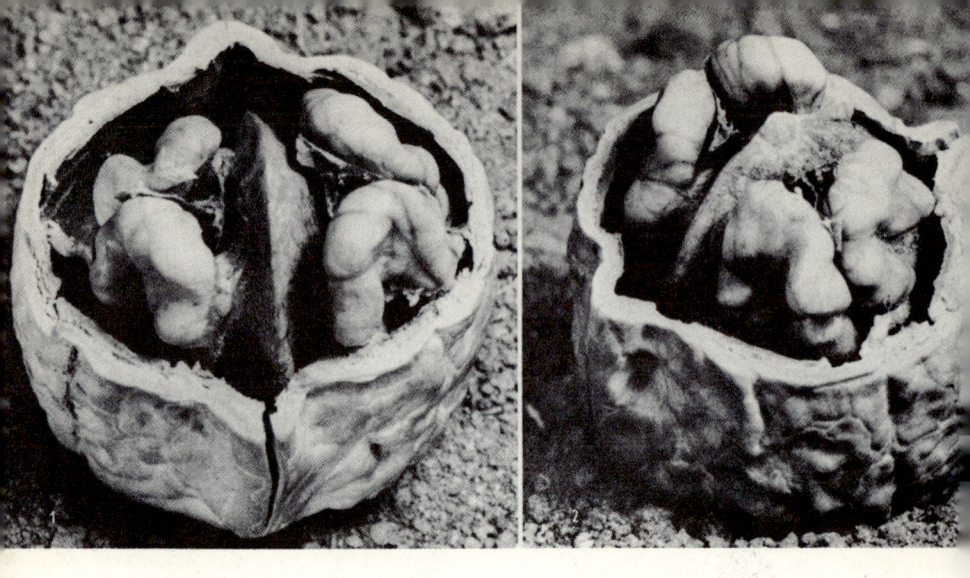

1 and 2. WALNUT SHELL, CUT CROSSWISE

The walnut shell is formed of two woody valves joined at their rims. It encloses a large seed, the edible part of the walnut. It owes its irregular shape to the first two leaves of the plantlet, the cotyledons, here still swollen and curiously deformed by food reserves. Each valve of the shell protects a cotyledon.

Illus. 1. In this view of the two halves of the shell along its axis, one cotyledon can be seen to the right, the other to the left.

Illus. 2. Turning the shell, we can see one cotyledon at the front, the other at the back. Each is divided on the outside into two distorted lobes. The cotyledons are joined where the valves divide. They form the body of

Between its two halves, the dry walnut

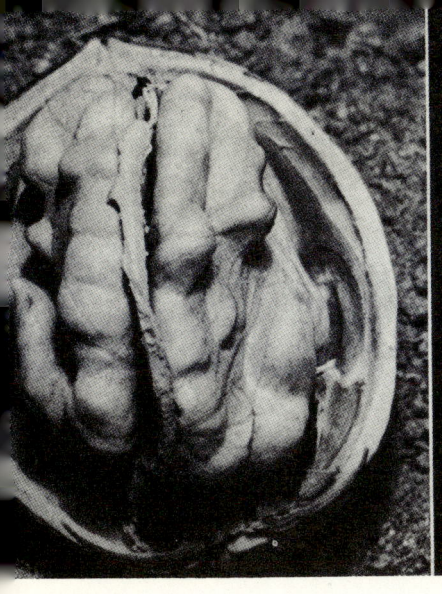

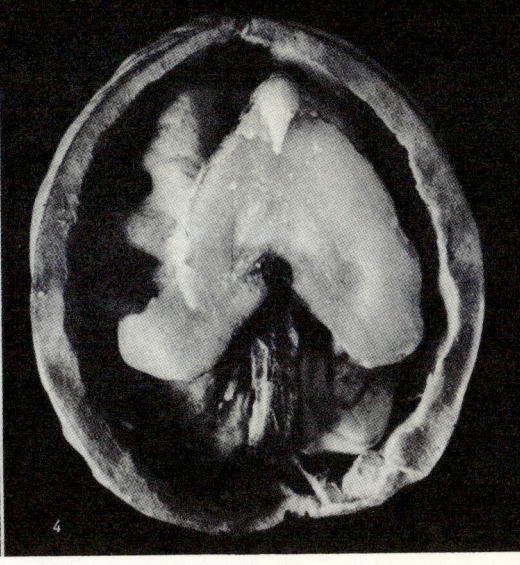

3. OPEN WALNUT   4. SECTION OF THE SEED

the seed, which is flattened and has sharp edges. The rest of the embryo is lodged in the tip of this central part. (See Illus. 4.)

Illus. 3. When one valve of the shell is removed, we can see the two lobes of a cotyledon, separated by a woody division.

Illus. 4. One cotyledon has been removed. The surface which joined it to the other one appears as a light-colored mass, shaped like an inverted heart. At its tip is the seed germ, which looks like a short finger pointing downward. It is hard to see the outline of the organs. The short, thick radicle points backward in the photograph; the thinner plumule points downward.

encloses an irregularly-shaped seed.

1. GERMINATING WALNUT   2. WITH THE SOIL REMOVED

Germination takes place in the same way as in the other trees. Notice the short but powerful young shoot.

The seed becomes a strong plant that

3. WALNUT PLANT IN THE AUTUMN, AFTER GERMINATION

The shoot soon grows longer. The cotyledons remain enclosed in the seed.

splits the two halves of the walnut shell.

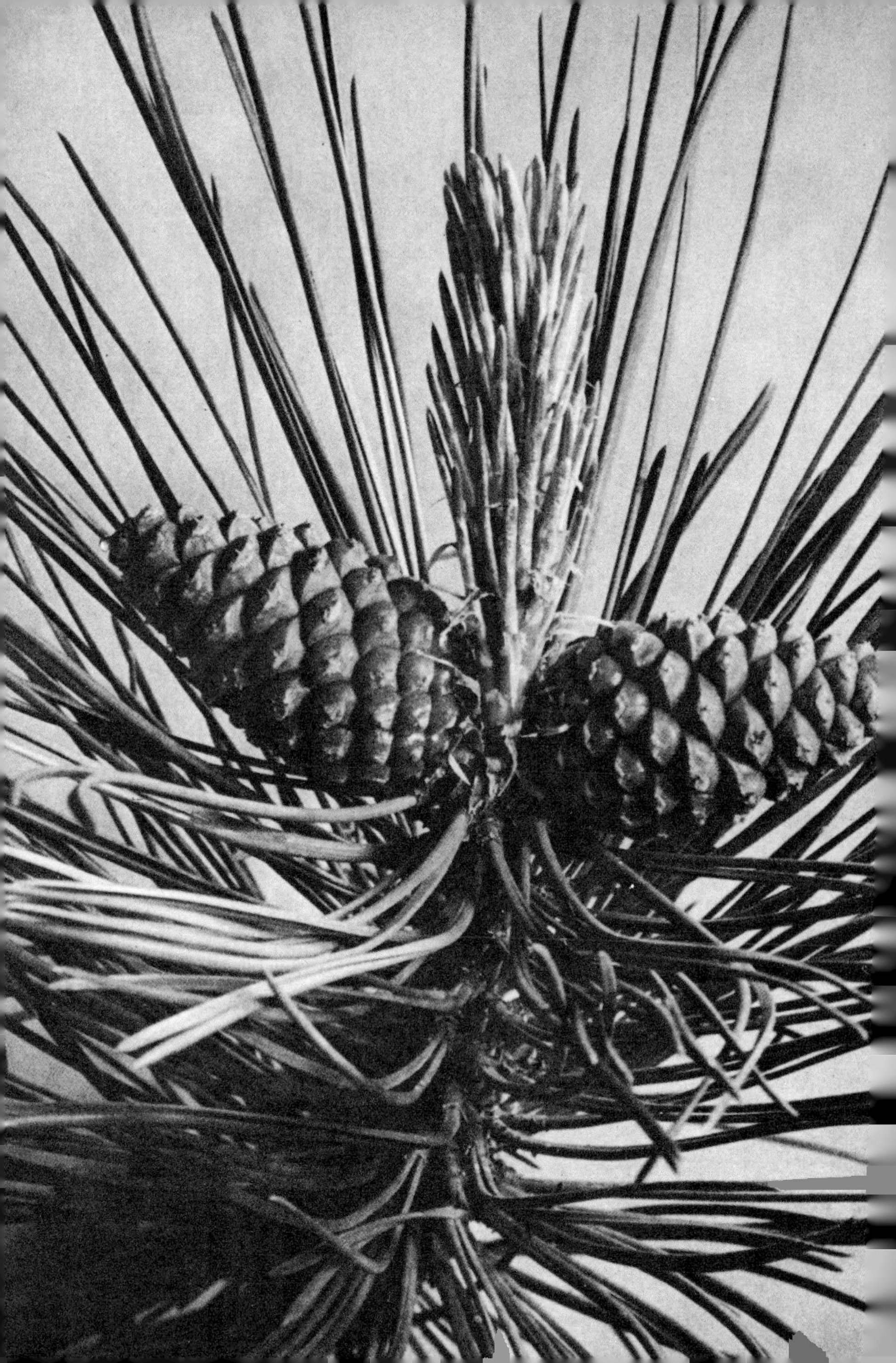

THE PINE TREE

Summer and winter, the pine tree

1. BLACK PINE   2. PINE BRANCHES

There are many species of pine trees. They differ in size, in appearance, in the shape and arrangement of their needles and cones, and so forth. The type shown here is a black pine, a large tree with a straight trunk that can reach a height of 110 feet. Its mass of foliage in outline against the sky forms the shape of a pyramid.

The trunk bears many branches which in turn branch and eventually form twigs with leaves at their tips. The leaves appear in tufts.

keeps its dark green leaves.

1. TIP OF A BRANCH IN EARLY SPRING
2. A NEW SHOOT IN LATER SPRING

Illus. 1. The pine is an evergreen; its leaves do not fall in autumn. They remain attached to the branch for several years (usually two or three years and up to seven years in some species). They are long, stiff, thin, and sharp; we call them pine needles. In the black pine, the needles are grouped by two's. Each pair grows from a very short twig. The terminal bud at the top of the twig will soon lengthen it.

Illus. 2. The terminal bud has opened and a leafy shoot is growing. Its needles, still pale and very small, completely mask the stalk. The previous year's

The leaves, in the shape of needles, remain

3. YOUNG NEEDLES
4. OLD BRANCH LOSING ITS LEAVES

shoot has long, darker needles.

Illus. 3. This is the base of a new but more advanced shoot. The first pair of needles, on the left, belong to the previous year's growth. All the others belong to the young shoot. Each pair is covered by a long thin, translucent sheath or covering. When the needles have reached their full size, the shriveled remains of this sheath can still be seen at their base.

Illus. 4. Finally, after several years, the needles die and fall, each pair breaking off the branch together with the short twig which bears them.

attached to the branches for several years.

1. NEW SHOOT AND MALE CONES
2. NEW SHOOT AND FEMALE CONES

Illus. 1. During May and June reproductive organs appear on some new shoots. These organs, which are called cones, have a special structure. The male cones are joined in small clusters *at the base* of the young shoots.

They are yellowish-green and measure about $\frac{3}{4}''$ to $1\frac{1}{4}''$. They are made up of many stamens which fit tightly over each other and produce a lot of very light pollen.

Illus. 2. Other shoots have one, two or three female cones *at their tip*. There is only one cone in this

(slightly enlarged)

Some new shoots bear male cones,

3. TWO FEMALE CONES
4. SECTION OF A FEMALE CONE

(magnified 3½ times)

picture. The female cones are reddish-brown and slightly smaller than the male cones.

Illus. 3 and 4. The female cone is made of scales arranged in a spiral around an axis. Each scale has two ovules on its upper surface (see page 90). The wind carries the pollen from the male to the female cones. Some grains of pollen, passing between two of the scales, reach the ovules. After pollination the cone will develop into the brown woody structure familiar to us as the pine cone. This transformation takes place very slowly over two years.

others tiny female cones.

1. SHOOT AND FEMALE CONES IN SPRING
2. SHOOT AND FEMALE CONES IN AUTUMN

These two pictures, slightly reduced, show the growth during the first year of a whole shoot bearing two female cones. In spring, its short needles make it easily recognizable. By autumn, the axis of the shoot has grown longer; the needles, fully grown, resemble those of the year before. A winter bud has formed between the two cones. The branch is ready to face the rigors of the winter season.

Pollinated in spring, the female cones

have grown a little by autumn.

1 and 2. DEVELOPMENT OF THE BRANCH AND CONES DURING THE SECOND YEAR

Illus. 1. In June of the second year, this is how the same branch looks. The long needles at the bottom were at the top of the shoot during the previous spring and autumn. The two large cones on the right and left of the branch are the same ones which enclosed the terminal bud in autumn. That bud has sprouted the short-needled young shoot on top. The new shoot itself has two small cones ready to receive pollen.

Illus. 2. In October the new shoot has reached its maximum size. Last year's cones are now ripe pine cones.

During the second year

the cones complete their growth.

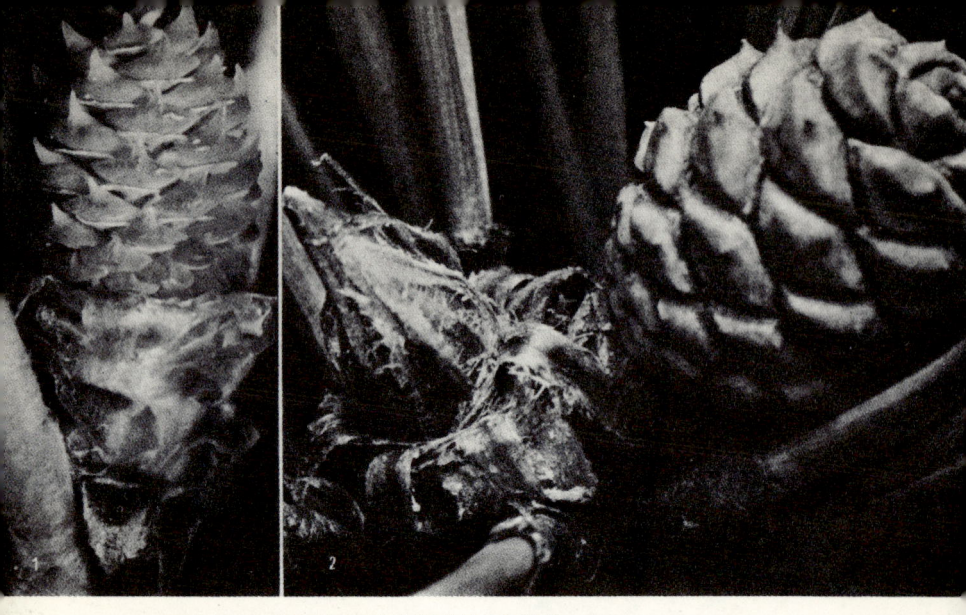

1 to 4. DEVELOPMENT OF THE FEMALE CONE

The pictures on the opposite page (and the two enlarged on this page) show the female cone at the following times: in spring of the first year (Illus. 1); in March of the second year (Illus. 2); in June (Illus. 3); and finally in autumn of the second year (Illus. 4).

During the first year, the female cone has grown slightly larger. Its scales, thickened and hardened, no longer have any space between them (Illus. 2). In this way the cone has passed through the winter. Its growth will start again at the same time as that of the bud on its left.

During the second year the most striking changes in size and shape take place (Illus. 3 and 4). By autumn the female cone has become woody and mature.

The tiny reddish cone then becomes

a fat pine cone, green and shining.

(magnified 5 times)

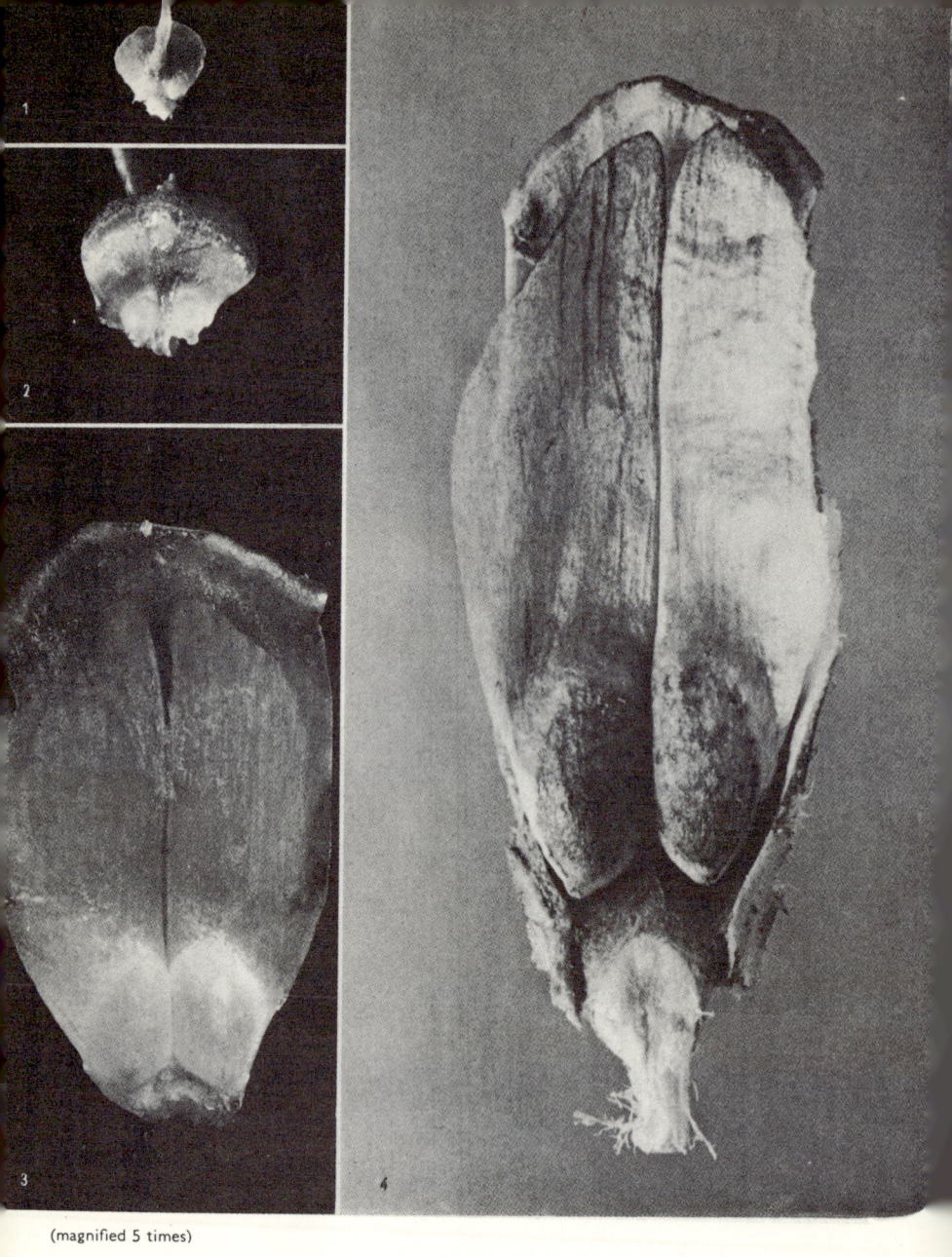

Each scale of the cone carries two ovules.

1 to 4. TRANSFORMATION OF THE OVULES INTO SEEDS
5. SCALE OPENS IN THE RIPE CONE
6. SECTION OF THE CONE SHOWING THE GROWTH OF A SEED

Illus. 1 to 4 show the upper surface of a scale torn from a female cone. We can retrace its development from spring to autumn of the first year (Illus. 1 and 2), and from spring to autumn of the second year (Illus. 3 and 4). There are two ovules at the base of the scale. Each of them becomes a seed with a large paper-thin wing (Illus. 4). This wing gradually forms from the outer tissues of the scale. When ripe, the seed gets ready to fall (Illus. 5 and 6).

Each ovule forms a winged seed.

The dry pine cone releases its seeds

1. PINE CONE EMPTIED OF ITS SEEDS
2. SEED DETACHED FROM THE CONE
3. SEEDS THAT HAVE LOST THEIR WINGS
4. SEEDS OF THE BLACK PINE SPROUTING

Though ripe by autumn, the pine cone sometimes will not release its seeds until the following spring. Then, when the air is dry, the scales of the cone separate and the winged seeds drop out. The empty cones may remain attached to the branch for several years. The seeds are carried only a short distance by the wind before their fragile wings fall off because of dampness. The wingless seeds continue on alone. They will germinate in spring if conditions are favorable.

We can more easily see the huge seeds of the stone pine than the smaller seeds of the black pine. The following pages show the structure of that seed and the way it germinates.

which will germinate in the following spring.

The seed, with woody skin, contains an embryo

1. SEEDS OF THE STONE PINE
2. SEED WITH ITS SKIN REMOVED
3. SEED TAKEN FROM ITS SKIN AND OPENED

Illus. 2. The skin of the seed is a thick and woody shell.* The central, living part of the seed is covered with a thin tissue that is separated from the inner surface of this shell.

Illus. 3. The seed contains an embryo surrounded by nutritive tissue. It differs from the other species in that the food reserves are not in the cotyledons but in a special tissue which is outside the embryo and completely envelops it. (Do not confuse this nutritive tissue, seen here in section, with the skin of the seed in the previous picture.) The many cotyledons are not deformed, but have the characteristic shape of pine leaves. They are inserted in the shape of a crown around the tip of the axis.** At the center of the crown there is a terminal bud that cannot be seen in the picture.

* This shell, which is the seed coat, is not like the hard shell of a nut, such as the walnut shell, which is formed by the inner wall of the fruit.
** The picture shows an embryo in which the cotyledons have been separated in order to make them clearer. In their natural state they are pressed close against each other, tightly compressed by the nutritive tissue.

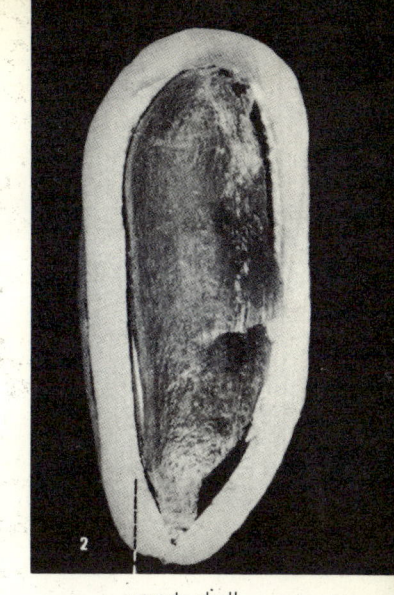

woody shell

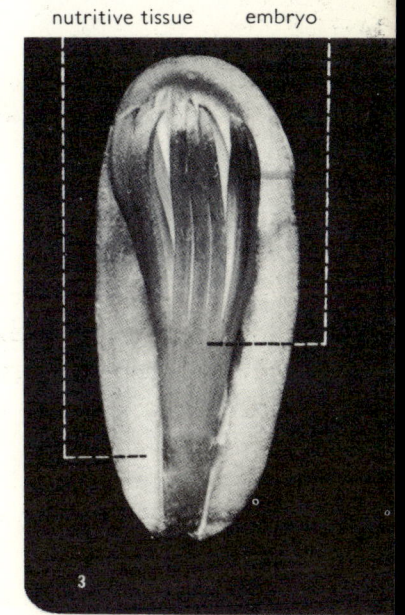

nutritive tissue   embryo

(magnified $2\frac{1}{2}$ times)

surrounded by tissue (which feeds it).

95

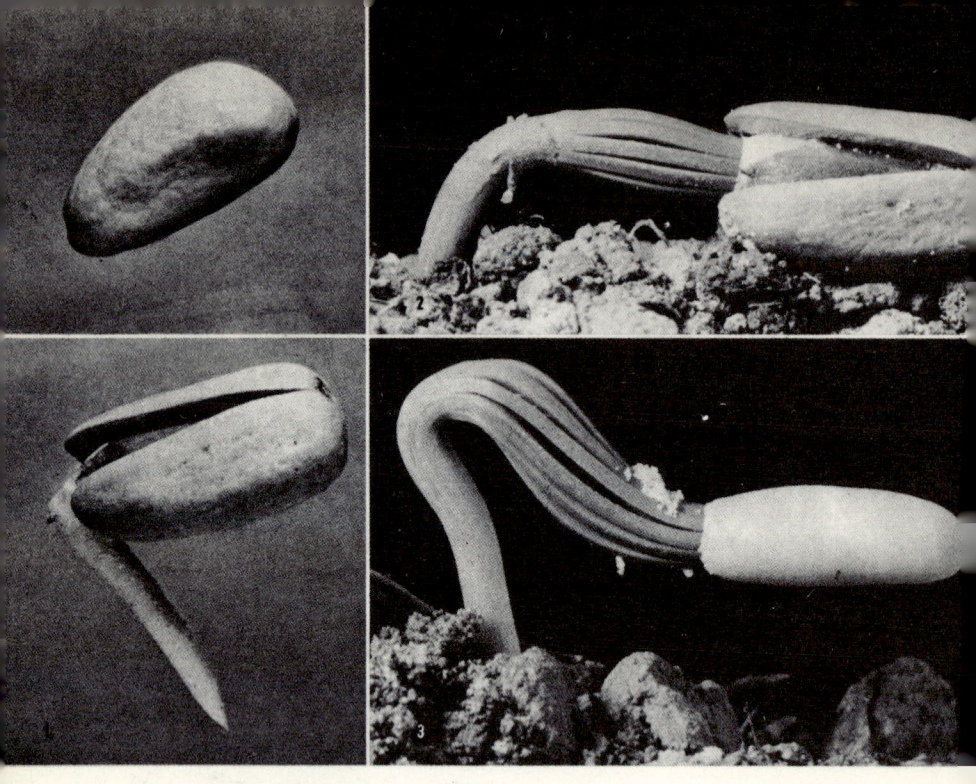

1 to 5. GERMINATION OF THE STONE PINE

In spring the shell breaks under internal pressure and the seed germinates. Germination differs in some details from that of the preceding trees. The cotyledons do not remain enclosed in the seed but gradually break away as they grow (Illus. 2, 3 and 4). The axis grows sufficiently to lift them some distance above the soil. The main axis of the seedling arises from the center of this cluster of cotyledons.

The plantlet takes root, lengthens its main axis,

releases and unfolds its leaves. A pine is born.

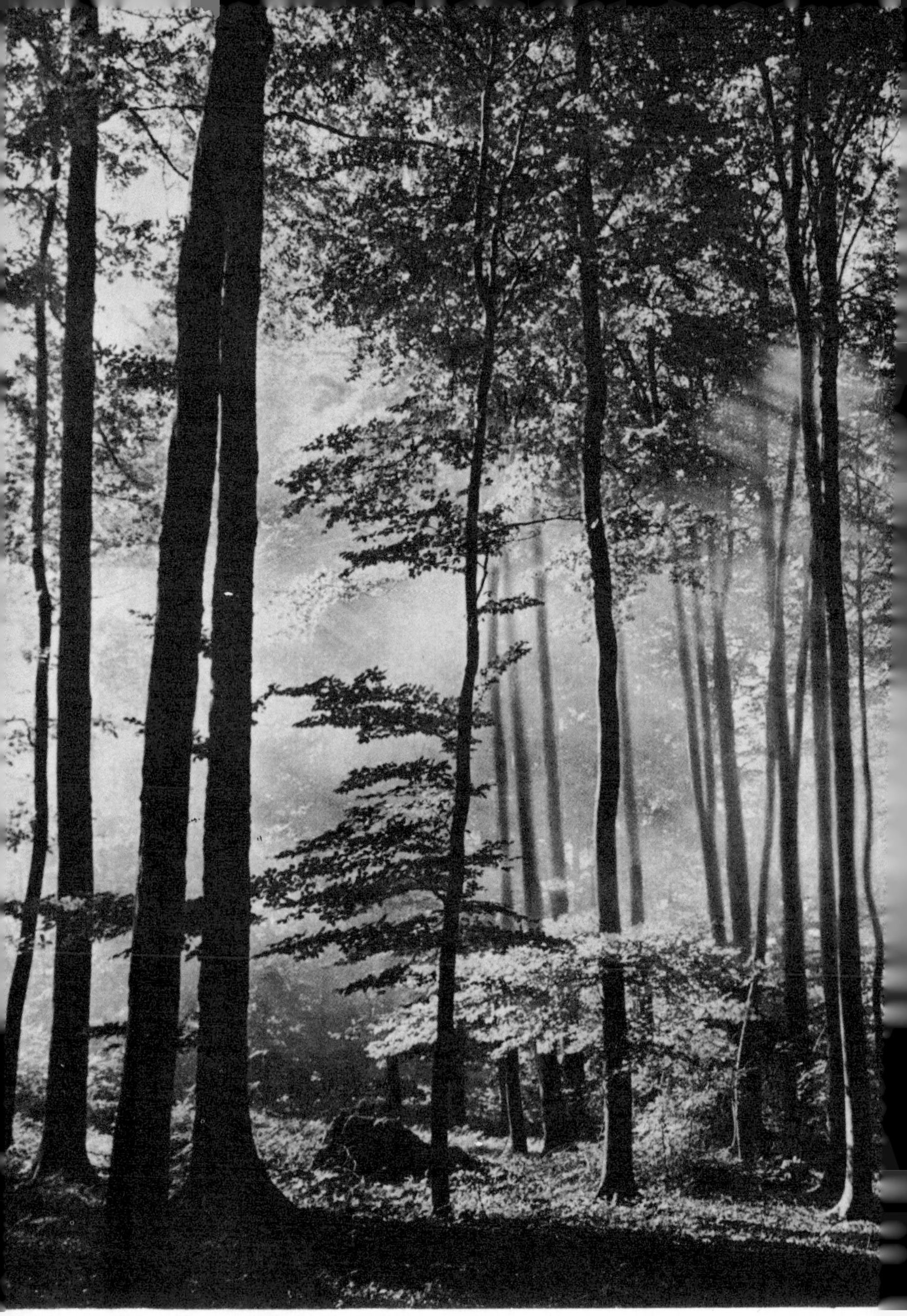

The seed germinates. A tiny tree is born. Its root, deeply buried, draws nourishment from the earth. Its stalk, already woody, no longer needs to fear the teeth of animals. Other dangers still threaten the young plant. Water can run short, the shade from older, taller plants can weaken it. However, each year that passes increases its chances of survival. Each spring the main stem will lengthen and a new ring of wood will thicken it. Little by little the plant will become a robust tree with a stout trunk.

In April each green shoot will give rise to branches. In October the older branches will lose their leaves, never to bear other leaves or flowers. But the leafless branches remain alive and other branches will grow from their buds. The older parts of the tree will store up the reserves necessary for new growth and will provide the sap. At last, thicker and stronger from year to year, the trunk and its branches will become part of that massive scaffolding that supports the huge dome of foliage. Worn out or full of youth, depending on the season, passing through a hundred eclipses and a hundred reawakenings, the tree will, if fortune favors it, reach old age: two or three hundred years for most species, eight hundred for some firs, many more for cedars and for the California sequoias. Mature sequoias, three hundred feet high, probably the oldest living things in the world, for two thousand years and more have followed this same rhythm.

Junior High School Library
Bremen, Indiana